# You Are Somebody

## You're Worth
## More Than You Think!

# You Are Somebody

## You're Worth
## More Than You Think!

*by*
*Cheryl*
*Miss America 1980*

Praise
BOOKS

A Division of Harrison House Publishers
Tulsa, Oklahoma

*2nd Printing*

*You Are Somebody!*
ISBN 0-89274-475-8
Copyright © 1988 by Cheryl Prewitt-Salem
P. O. Box 701287
Tulsa, OKlahoma 74170

Published by Praise Books
A Division of Harrison House Publishers
P. O. Box 35035
Tulsa, Oklahoma 74153

# Contents

I would like to express my thanks to Jeanne Alcott for her work in preparing this book.

I appreciate her willingness to allow God to flow through me into her. She lost her identity and actually became me to help write this book.

# Preface

I know when you picked up this book, the thought probably flashed through your mind: "How can a Miss America help me with my self-image? Of course, she has a good self-image. Who wouldn't, being Miss America?"

Well, I've got good news for you: the fact that I have a good self-image is the reason why I can help you. Because so many bad things have happened to me in every facet of my life, I could never have gotten from where I was to where I am now if I had had a bad self-image. But through God in me, I overcame all those obstacles that could have dragged me down and kept me living in poverty in Choctaw County, Mississippi, where I grew up in a poor house on a dirt road.

No matter why you have a bad self-image, believe me, I can help you. If anyone deserved to have a bad self-image and not work for a good one, it was me. If your problem is physical, I can help you, because I have been through two terrible accidents. One left me a cripple (with one leg two inches shorter than the other) and barren (with no hope, according to the doctors, of ever being able to bear a child of my own). Both accidents left my face badly scarred.

If your problem is emotional, I can help you because I have lived through physical tragedies that were just as detrimental to me emotionally as they were physically. Then when I began to compete in beauty pageants, I was rejected in pageant after pageant. A few years later, I suffered through an extremely difficult marriage which ended in an equally difficult divorce. But through everything — my childhood, my marriage, and my divorce — I came out victorious.

If your problem is financial, I can help you, because I grew up in a very poor family. Almost *everything* I wore in the beauty pageants was borrowed, especially in the first few years.

And if your problem is spiritual, I can help you. Through all my tests and trials, I learned how to come out on top with a good self-image and spiritually strong by *staying in the Word of God.*

Believe me, I've been through a lot, and that's why I wrote this book — to help you. That's why I can say to you that you can do anything, you can go anywhere, and you can become anything God wants you to be — if you are willing. In this book I have opened up my life as never before, but I didn't stop there. I have given you very practical helps and guidelines for you to use in improving your self-image.

Everybody has a self-image — it's either bad or good. If yours is bad, I can help you learn how to develop a good one. If yours is already good, I can help you learn how to improve it even more so that you can reach your fullest potential!

You can never start too soon or too late to develop a good self-image. Teenage years are some of the most important in the formation of a good self-image. But if you're older and you're thinking, "It's too late for me to try to change my self-image," all I can say to you is, you have more ahead of you than behind you.

Well, are you ready? Believe me, it will be well worth everything you put into learning who you are and what you can become with a good self-image!

# 1
# Miss America
# in Spite of It All

There I was — walking down the brilliantly lit runway with hot lights beaming on me, cameras flashing everywhere, with twenty-five thousand people watching there in Atlantic City and another 100 million watching by television in their homes.

I could feel the crown on my head that told the world I was now the new Miss America. As I stood there looking into a sea of people, with tears streaming down my face, my life seemed to pass before me. I saw where God had brought me from as I relived the hurts that had caused the wounds that were now scars, both physically and emotionally.

I had seen the worst and I had seen the best, and I liked the best. I liked walking in health.

You see, when I was eleven years old I was involved in a terrible car wreck which scarred my face for life and left me a cripple for many years. It happened one very normal, innocent day — May 4, 1968. My older sister had decided to pick up some tomato plants for Mama. And, of course, all of us kids wanted to go. So I grabbed up my two younger brothers and we all took off down the road in the family car.

To get the tomato plants, we had to drive to Chester, which was the nearest community to our home in rural Choctaw County, Mississippi, where I grew up.

It was as small as the name sounds, and the people living there had just enough means to get by one day at a time. Because I had never had much exposure to the world outside of Choctaw County, I did not realize how poor we really were. I mean, we were dirt poor.

Probably the best story I can give to illustrate just how poor we actually were is the one about the little Barbie doll that I once retrieved out of a trash can where it had been thrown away because a dog had bitten the arm off of it. But since it was the only Barbie doll I had ever had, I thought it was the most wonderful thing on earth. I didn't care if the doll's arm was gone and it was somebody else's "throw-away." I was just happy to have a real Barbie of my own.

But the beginning of the end to that simple little world I was living in came that day on our way to Chester. We were about a mile into our trip when we had to pass around a car that was parked in the road in front of a friend's house. It was a little narrow dirt road and there wasn't anywhere else to go, so we swerved to miss the parked car. As we did, we moved right into the path of an oncoming car. It belonged to our next-door neighbor who had been out buying groceries. When the cars both got to the top of a rise in the road, they hit head-on.

The impact of hitting another car head-on not only caused my face to hit the windshield, it also drove the engine of our car through the dashboard where it landed right in my lap. I'll never forget how sick I felt after I became conscious and looked at my left leg. It was so crushed above the knee that the skin on the front and back literally touched like the material of a dress lying flat. There simply was not any bone left above my knee. But the worst part of the entire accident was the fact that the mother of our next-door neighbor's family died right there at the side of the road.

I remember when my mama and daddy arrived at the scene of the accident. They were almost in shock as they put all of us kids in a neighbor's car and drove us to the nearest hospital. We groaned and cried all the way there because of the injuries we had all suffered — it was the worst trip of our lives.

When we finally arrived at the hospital, the doctors put over 100 stitches in my face and then just stopped counting. There were so many lacerations they couldn't possibly count all the stitches! After they finished in the emergency room, I was given a mirror. When I looked in it, I thought my face looked like something out of a horror movie.

I was then placed in traction, not only because of my crushed leg, but because the doctors had discovered that my back had been cracked in the accident. When they finished their work, all I could move was my head, and that only from side to side. But the worst was yet to come.

Unfortunately, at the hospital in little Webster County, an adjoining county to Choctaw, there wasn't much more they could do for me. So a few weeks later, I was transferred by ambulance to a hospital in Columbus, about fifty miles away. There, Dr. Sanders, the best orthopedic surgeon in Mississippi, performed surgery on my leg. Afterwards he wrapped me in an eighty-pound plaster-of-Paris cast that stretched from my chest to my toes on the left side and from my chest to my knee on the right side. It was then that I had to come to terms with what had happened to me.

When I looked in the mirror, I didn't see anything pretty — everything was ugly and defeated. But God began to show me that what I was on the outside was nothing; all that mattered was what I was on the inside. And if I would center in on the inside, He would take care of the outside.

So at eleven years of age I decided to go to God. As I began to spend time with Him and let Him feed me spiritually, I began to change on the inside. Although I had grown up in a precious little church, I had never been taught anything about healing. Even my mama and daddy didn't know anything about it. But, believe me, if you know that the only way you are ever going to walk again is to be healed by God, then you'll find out what *He* thinks about healing.

It didn't matter to me that many of my relatives and friends told me things like, "You've got to get this notion out of your head. God is not going to heal you, Honey. The doctors have said that you will never walk again." It didn't matter what they thought of me. All that mattered was what I thought of me, and that's when my life took a turning point — when I learned *faith*.

I had child-like faith and I understood the principles involved. I understood that God is all-powerful and that He is like a father. I knew that Luke 11:13 says that if our earthly fathers want to give us good things, how much more does He, our heavenly Father, want to give us good things! As I watched my earthly father and mother cry and weep as all four of their children lay hurting in that hospital after the accident, wanting us all well, I knew that God, my heavenly Father, wanted me well too.

So with my little heart full of faith, I went to the Lord with all the boldness I could muster and said, "God, I don't know how You do this kind of thing, but I want You to heal me."

From the moment I asked Him to heal me, I believed He would. And, as I began to set my belief in motion, the Father began to do His work. A cocoon of bone began to manifest itself, just wrapping up and down inside my left leg. At the end of three months' time, when they cut the body cast off of me and stood me up to examine my left leg, the doctors declared my recovery a miracle. They said the bone in my left leg was the strongest one in my entire body.

But because I was eleven years old and still growing, my right leg had grown almost two inches longer than my left one. But that was okay with me because I was just happy to have two legs that would work. I didn't care if one was a little different from the other. I was just glad I could walk.

School was starting soon, so Mama set about hemming the left leg of all my pants approximately two inches shorter than the right leg. And off to school I went. My friends declared me a cripple, but I declared myself a miracle. And that's what made the difference — the way I saw myself, not the way *they* saw me.

I knew inside me that God was powerful and strong and that He could overcome. So I began to center in on what God could do in my life and began to grow up in Him. Then, at fourteen years of age, I asked Jesus into my heart as my Lord and my Savior.

Now you may be thinking, "Wait a minute. You asked God to heal you, and He did. And then, three years later, you became a Christian?"

That is absolutely right.

Even though I was healed, I had not fully accepted Jesus Christ as my Savior. You see, I grew up in the South at a time when everybody went to church. It didn't matter what you did the rest of the week, you had just better go to church on Sunday. And I went to church every Sunday morning, every Sunday night, and every Wednesday night, so I knew a lot *about* God. I knew everything the Father had done for me by sending His only Son to die for me. I knew everything Jesus had done for me by dying on the cross for my sins. But I didn't *know* the Father, and I didn't *know* Jesus.

It was then that God the Father began to speak in my heart and let me know, "You know all about Me, but you don't know Me. You know all about My Son Jesus, but you don't know My Son Jesus."

When He began to show me this, I thought, "You know, that is the difference between knowing all about the President of the United States and actually knowing the President himself."

Right then I had a personal encounter with the Father and I asked Him to be my Lord and my Savior. It was then that He began to work in my heart and to move inside me — but that was *not* the end of my problems.

Three years later, when I was seventeen years old, my doctor told me that I would have problems later on in life. He was talking about how damaged the inside of my body was, along with my hips, as a result of the accident. And because of that damage, I would not be able to have any children.

Well, I had learned through those six years since my accident to never panic, just to go to God's Word and find out what He has to say about the situation. So I studied the Bible and found scriptures like the one in which Jesus said:

> **Verily, verily, I say unto you, He that believeth on me, the works that I do shall he do also; and greater works than these shall he do; because I go unto my Father.**
>
> **And whatsoever ye shall ask in my name, that will I do, that the Father may be glorified in the Son.**
>
> **John 14:12-13**

And I thought, "Well, Lord, You say that we can do what You did, but what all did You do? I can only believe in what You did if I know what You did."

So I went back through the books of Matthew, Mark, Luke and John and found out real quick that one of the great works Jesus did was *healing lame legs.* When I saw that, I thought, "That's for me. That's all it takes."

But I realized I had to find out the "how." So I kept reading the Bible, and I discovered Jesus' words in Matthew 18:18,19:

> **Verily I say unto you, Whatsoever ye shall bind on earth shall be bound in heaven: and whatsoever ye shall loose on earth shall be loosed in heaven.**

> **Again I say unto you, That if two of you shall agree on earth as touching any thing that they shall ask, it shall be done for them of my Father which is in heaven.**

I thought, "If the Bible says that *two* of us should agree, then the more people the better, so I'll just get a hundred to agree with me!"

So I asked just about everybody I knew to agree with me in prayer that I was going to be healed *completely!* Then I read Mark 11:23 in which Jesus said:

> **For verily I say unto you, That whosoever shall say unto this mountain, Be thou removed, and be thou cast into the sea; and shall not doubt in his heart, but shall believe that those things which he saith shall come to pass; he shall have whatsoever he saith.**

As I began to see this principle and grasp hold of it, I became more and more hungry to learn. Then I found out that according to my faith, so it would be unto me. (Matt. 9:29.) And I said, "Lord, how do I have faith?"

The Lord said to me, "Faith comes by hearing, and hearing by the Word of God." (Rom. 10:17.)

I thought, "All right then, if the Word of God is how I get faith, then I will just read the Word to myself."

So I would just open the Bible at any point and I would start reading the Word to myself. Then I decided to read it out loud because if I read it aloud I would hear it, and if I heard it, it would get down into my heart, and the Bible says that . . . **out of the abundance of the heart the mouth speaketh** (Matt. 12:34).

As I did this, I discovered that this is the way it goes: You get the Word of God down in your heart, and then it comes out of your mouth, and when it comes out of your mouth, it gets in your ears. Then the whole cycle starts again — out of your mouth and into your ears; into your ears and down into your heart; down into your heart and out of our mouth; out of your mouth and into your ears . . . . Before you know it, you've got a good cycle of faith going in your life. And I knew that *faith* was what I had to have in order to be healed.

I, especially, liked to read the Bible on the days when the devil was hanging around and would not leave me alone. I had to show him who was boss, so on those days I would say, "Devil, just pull up a chair. I believe I will read to you today." I would open the Bible and I'd start reading to him. He didn't like that very much, so I'd read some more. Then I would read louder and louder and louder, and it wouldn't be very long before he was gone. The devil didn't like the Word of God then, and he still doesn't like it!

So I was reading the Word and hearing the Word, and my faith was getting stronger. About three months passed with my doing this. Then the fateful day came.

I had been teaching piano lessons for a while when the mother of one of my students asked if I wanted to attend a meeting in which an evangelist named Kenneth Hagin was going to be speaking on faith. I had never heard of him (he wasn't well known in my little church) but when he came to town, I went to hear him. I had never been to a service like that one. It seemed as though everyone there had his "faith out" and was hungry and ready for God to move in his life. I believe God's anointing was already on the place before we ever even did anything.

At the end of the service, Brother Hagin asked if anybody in the audience wanted to receive his healing. Well, I was ready! I went right down to the front of the auditorium where many of the people were standing in line waiting for Brother Hagin to lay his hands on them and pray for them.

As I stood there, I heard Brother Hagin say, "Just get your mind, and your eyes and ears, off of everybody, including yourself. Just close your eyes and center on the Father."

As I did what Brother Hagin suggested, I saw the Father sitting on the throne with His Son Jesus beside Him. As I saw them in my spirit, I said, "Lord, I just want You to give me anything and everything You want me to have."

As soon as I said that, I began to feel the arms of God the Father and Jesus the Son reach out to me. They were different arms, but the same person — it was as if they were one. They reached out, brought me up into their arms and just whispered into my ear, "Child, We've been waiting for you."

And when the Lord spoke those words to me, just like that, my left leg grew out to the same length as my right leg!

That was when it all started happening for me. Although I had never lifted my hands in a service, I lifted them then because it just felt like the thing to do. Suddenly I began to speak in another language. I thought, "Father, You've given just me a whole precious gift." I thought I was the only one who had this gift. I didn't know that many thousands of others had it too! Later I found out that I had received an *infilling* of the Holy Ghost, one of the Holy Trinity, and that He *was* just for me, as He is just for you and each of God's children.

That was the beginning of the "fuel" for my "tank." And my tank got fuller and fuller and fuller. And as it did, I started praying and asking God, "What do You want me to do with my life? God, I don't want to make a move without You. Tell me what to do, and I will do it."

He answered me. Six months after I was healed, He said, "I want you to be in pageants."

So I went running home and told my daddy, "God has called me into pageants."

I'll bet that right now you are laughing. Well, that's just about how my daddy reacted. He really thought I had lost my mind. We talked back and forth until finally Daddy said, "All right, Cheryl, I'm not going to argue with you. You can go and be in those pageants, but I'm not going to help you, and I'm not going to go to any of them. In fact, I don't want to have any part of them; but I'll do one thing, I'll give you my permission to enter."

I thought, "God, this is wonderful. You've given me direction and Daddy has given me permission, but there is just one small problem — in Choctaw County there are no pageants for me to enter! I mean, I've got to enter something in order to win!"

But I just kept praying and believing and soon for the first time in many years Choctaw County held a Miss Choctaw County Pageant. And, of course, I just knew that God had made it happen just for me!

I entered the Miss Choctaw County Pageant, not knowing one thing about pageants. I didn't know how to walk properly. (I was just happy to be walking.) I didn't know how to talk properly. (You can imagine how a young country girl talked who grew up eight miles from the nearest town, which had only 2,000 people in it — and from Mississippi to boot!) I didn't know how to put on makeup or how to dress properly. I mean, I didn't know *anything* about the whole setup of pageants. I just thought that if God had called me, that was enough.

The time for the pageant came and the first thing we contestants had to do was to be interviewed by the judges. As I went to my interview the afternoon of the pageant, I thought I would just go in there in front of the judges and that would be it — everything would be great!

I walked to the door that led to where the interview was to take place. There in front of the door stood a sweet little lady who tapped each contestant on the head as she went in and said, "Just go in there and be yourself." That turned out to be the worst advice anybody has ever given me! I went in there and I was just *myself*.

As I answered the interview questions, the judges began to laugh. Well, I had believed so hard and my faith was so high that I took their reaction to mean that I was doing real good. So I just kept going in that same manner — just really rolling! The more they laughed, the more I was convinced I was doing good. One judge laughed so hard he got down off his chair and beat the floor with his fist! So when the interview was over, I just *knew* I had the pageant won.

That evening the pageant began with the talent competition, followed by the evening gown competition, and closing with the swimsuit competition. Finally the big moment arrived and the master of ceremonies began calling out all the names of the runners-up, and guess what? I came in first runner-up.

I mean, I was disgusted. Now most people would think, "That's great, getting first runner-up." But I thought, "God, You have called me, but I've lost. I don't care which runner-up I am, I have lost. I have not won."

The Lord and I had a discussion about the situation, and He began to show me just one little minor point that I had missed: *I had gone into that pageant totally and completely unprepared!*

You know, that is the way many people are. God calls them to do something, and they think they can just run and jump in with both feet, and everything will be fine. They don't see the need to prepare. The Lord showed me that after the call is placed on your life, then comes a time of preparation. The preparation is as vitally important as the call.

You see, God loves us so much that He wants you and me to be the very best. He wants us to be prepared. He wants us to know who we are. He wants us to be driven and determined and to have a good self-image so we can become all that we can possibly be.

So I repented of not being prepared and asked God to forgive me. And because He is so full of grace and love, He did forgive me. Soon I started working toward the Miss Mississippi State University Pageant the next year. As I did, I thought, "Lord, I will be the most prepared pageant person in Your entire kingdom, and I *will* be ready."

I worked harder and borrowed prettier clothes than the first year. I just got everything I could working together in my favor.

When I went to my second pageant, my faith was high and I thought, "You know, first runner-up isn't so bad. Just one more step and I'll be the winner." Well, the master of ceremonies called out the names of all the runners-up, and guess what? Not only did I not win, but I came in *second* runner-up!

I still believed that God had called me, so I went back the third year and, to make a long story short, that year I came in *third* runner-up!

Believe it or not, my fourth year in pageants I went back to try again to win the title of Miss Mississippi State, and that year I finally won my first local pageant. Oh, I praised God and thanked Him for everything He had done and how He had brought me to this point and had given me favor to last this long.

Then off I went to the Miss Mississippi Pageant just full of faith that I was going to be the next Miss Mississippi. The pageant week went by quickly and before I knew it I was standing among the top ten contestants on the final evening. The master of ceremonies called out the names of the runners-up and, you guessed it. I came in *first runner-up*.

I thought, "Oh God, I've been here before. And I well remember what follows!" I knew God knew all things, but I thought maybe I should just remind Him that these pageants did have an age limit, you know!

Now an important point to make here is this — if I had had a bad self-image, I would have quit during this discouraging time. I mean, going through that many times of losing was downright disheartening! Right after I lost the Miss Mississippi Pageant, I had decided that this must not be God's will for me and that I should just quit — *but* I knew in my heart I was supposed to be in pageants so I kept entering them and I kept feeling God's direction in it all. I knew that, lose or not, there was a reason for it all, so I stayed with it.

It's a good self-image like I had that will keep you going when things don't turn out exactly as you think they should. That is why it is so important to have a good image of yourself — because things are not always going to happen according to your plans, and a good self-image can help you through those hard times. You've got to have "stick-to-it-ive-ness."

Sometimes things don't happen when you think they should, but many times there is a good reason for the time lapse — and it's always for *your* good. Always remember that. It's not for somebody else's good that these things happen to you. It's for *your* good. Keep that in mind and you can maintain your good self-image. That's what kept me going — even when my family didn't support me. But I knew God would take care of that, and He did at that Miss Mississippi Pageant.

It was the first pageant my dad had ever attended. (Mama made him go.) Well, during the pageant he decided to share Jesus with the man sitting beside him, and when he did, that man received Jesus as his Savior. Afterwards Daddy came running up to me and told me what had happened. Then he said, "God's in pageants and everything is great."

I thought back to the time when I had told Daddy I felt that God wanted me to be in pageants and how he had rejected the idea. But I knew God would work it all out with Daddy if I was just patient — and He did.

By this time, I had graduated from Mississippi State University, and I was concerned because I still had not fulfilled the vision God had given me in high school. The problem was that I could not enter the Miss Mississippi State University Pageant since I had been to the Miss Mississippi Pageant once already with that title. So I decided to enter the town pageant of Starkville (the city in which Mississippi State is located). It was my fifth year in pageants.

As I stood on stage the evening of the pageant, a now familiar feeling, I prayed a very simple but powerful prayer. I said, "Lord, if You can use me more as Miss Starkville than You can as just Cheryl Prewitt, I want to be Miss Starkville." And I won the Miss Starkville Pageant!

Six weeks later, once again I was at the Miss Mississippi Pageant. And once again my faith was high. I was believing, and I was prepared. There on the stage I prayed, "Lord, if You can use me more as Miss Mississippi than You can as Miss Starkville, I want to be Miss Mississippi." And I won the Miss Missisippi Pageant!

Six weeks later, I was in Atlantic City, New Jersey, in the Miss America Pageant. Believe me, I had already found myself a prayer that worked so I was sticking to it! As I stood on the stage with the top ten finalists, I prayed, "Lord, if You can use me more as Miss America, than You can as Miss Mississippi, I want to be Miss America."

Well, there we stood, all lined up as Bert Parks called out the names of the runners-up. First, he called out the fourth runner-up, and she came out of the line-up just as though she was as thrilled to be the fourth runner-up as anybody could be. But of course we all knew she was madder than a wet hen. (I knew she was, because I had been in her place.) Then Bert called out the third runner-up, and she did the same thing. Then he called out the second runner-up, and the first runner-up, and they took their positions. In the meantime, as each girl's name was called out, the rest of us who were left in the line-up moved closer and closer together, holding hands as though we were the best of friends! (I was on the end standing by Miss Iowa who seemed to me to be at least 6'6" tall, and I'm only about 5'5"!)

By this time five years had passed since the moment God had first given me the dream for my life. I was so sure I was supposed to be Miss America for the Father that I prayed, "Now Father, help me not to step out until Bert calls my name. Nobody would believe that You told me all this was going to happen!"

Well, you know the rest of the story. I walked that runway to be your Miss America, but mostly I was the Father's Miss America to once again prove that He is God and Lord of lords, and that He can take care of things — that He has not fallen off the throne.

As I went down the runway, about halfway down I thought of how many steps of my life the Father had led me through to get me to that point. As I began to talk to Him, I said, "Oh, thank You, thank You, Lord. My dream is here. The dream I've dreamed so long is now a reality. *Now* what do I do?"

My thoughts whirled around me. As I continued to walk down that runway (no, really float, because my feet never seemed to touch the floor), I could see my family, my friends, my pageant people; but most of all I saw faces — the faces of so many people who needed Jesus. Even though they were smiling on the outside, I knew they were hurting and crying on the inside. This stirred me so much that I prayed, "Jesus, help me carry the burden of these souls. Show me what to do."

Then I thought, "Lord, it would be real simple just to be a nice girl and wave and be nice to people, and if anybody asked about my faith, I could say, 'Yes, I'm a Christian,' and not make any waves."

But I heard the Lord's voice very strongly in my spirit say to me, "I didn't bring you to this point for that reason." Then He had me envision a little crippled girl from Choctaw County, Mississippi. He made me realize that had it not been for His power, that little crippled girl would now be at home watching the Miss America Pageant in a wheelchair instead of walking down that runway in the glare of the television lights.

I wept as I thought, "God, never let me doubt that You are the One I am to lift up, and show me when and how to lift You up."

So, as I stood on that runway, *I lifted up the Father.*

As soon as I walked off that runway, I went into my first press conference. I decided to just give the press the whole story just as it had happened. If giving my testimony as Miss America was going to cause problems for the pageant officials, I wanted to face that situation right then and get it settled. Fortunately, that was not the case. I was allowed complete freedom of expression.

So I just lifted up the Father. I told the press how the Lord had brought me all the way from poverty in Mississippi to a crown in Atlantic City. I told them how grateful I was to Him, how much He loves all people and how much He wants to do for all of us. I told them that Jesus is my Savior . . . He is Lord . . . He cares about our lives . . . He wants us to be filled with the Holy Ghost . . . and He wants us to be healed.

I thought, "I'll just lay it on them. They may as well get it all *now*."

The beauty of the press is that they will print the views of a Miss America, regardless of how they may feel about those views personally. So I just laid on them God's message to me about His love for all of His children and His plan for our lives — and they just wrote it all down and printed it! Praise God!

I saw then the reason for many of the years when I hadn't won. I saw all the knowledge I had gained through those years and how I had grown because of it. I realized that if I had become Miss America years before, I wouldn't have been able to handle it nearly as well or have realized the importance of it.

As I had victoriously struggled through those years of losing, I had discovered that every year I lost, Jesus became more and more the Lord of my life. And when I finally won, I was so conformed to God's will that it didn't bother me to lift up the Lord, no matter where I was. If it was in Atlantic City in a casino, or in California or Kansas or Texas, no matter where I was, I found out very quickly that I wanted Miss America to do one thing — lift up the Lord in places He may never be lifted up any other way.

When I did this, the Lord honored my obedience and many people received Him as their Savior — some were even healed!

Today I know that God brought me to the point of being Miss America so I could do what I am doing now. More than anything else, I believe He made me Miss America to demonstrate to you that if He can take me from Choctaw County, Mississippi, and make me Miss America, He can do absolutely anything with you. He can put you anywhere and cause you to become anything He needs you to be. God wanted me to be Miss America, and He proved He could do it, and there was not one thing the devil could do to stop it. We had beat the system — the world system!

One of the things the Lord has shown me is that He doesn't want us to be the greatest things on earth. All He ever wants from us is obedience and willingness. You see, obedience and willingness — that was all He needed from me. I didn't have to be the prettiest girl.

I didn't have to be the most talented girl. I didn't have to have anything going for me, except obedience and willingness, and because I had those two things, God could take me from where I was to where I am.

I want to encourage you because you do have a ministry of some kind. Where God has called me to go, nobody else can go. And where God has called you to go, nobody else can go. If you think, "God, I'm not good enough to work for You," or, "I don't have the ability to do what You've called me to do," or, "I can't begin today as You want me to because I'm too tired," I want you to know that those thoughts are lies from the devil.

Any thought that comes to your mind to try to stop you from doing what God has called you to do is a lie of the devil! He is trying to destroy your self-image, because he knows someone with a good self-image can do a lot for God.

That is what this book is all about — helping you to develop the self-image you want to have, and that God wants you to have, so you can become all that He wants you to be. As we talk about your self-image, I know that God is going to do tremendous things in you — more than you can ever imagine, more than you ever thought possible — because God says He does supernaturally far above and beyond that which we dare to ask or even think. (Eph. 3:20.) I don't know about you, but I can think pretty big. And I can even ask for a lot. But He says He gives superabundantly far above and beyond that!

Later in this book I'll be sharing with you more about my life and the problems I had growing up and

31

the problems I've had since my reign as Miss America, 1980 . . . and through them how I determined to have a good self-image . . . and how you can learn to have a better self-image and therefore a better, happier, and more successful life!

# 2
# Looking in the Mirror

At this point, I think it's very important to tell you that this book is an *active book*. It's a two-way street. I can communicate to you about your self-image, but if you don't communicate back to yourself, you won't be affected and your life won't be changed. That's why I've even included special worksheets for you to fill out, so you will be able to get feedback as to where you are and where you've got to go. So I encourage you to put your whole self into the wonderful change that is about to take place in you.

Before we get too far along, let's establish what a self-image is; then you can evaluate your own self-image. We'll look at who you are and who God wants you to be.

Webster defines *self-image* as "an individual's conception of himself and his own identity, abilities, worth, etc."[1] In other words, it's what we think and how we feel about ourselves — the way we see ourselves.

If you're thinking right now, "Well, I really don't have a self-image," yes you do! *Everyone* has a self-image, whether he realizes it or not. You may have a good self-image or a bad self-image, but like everyone else, you do have one.

---

[1] *Webster's New World Dictionary of the American Language: Second College Edition* (New York and Cleveland: The World Publishing Company, 1970), p. 1292.

No one can totally not think anything about himself or herself. We all think something about ourselves, and we all have some kind of idea of what we're like as individuals, whether we like what we think we are or not.

A self-image is a lot like the reflection in a mirror. What we see in the mirror is an image. Our self-image is constantly being affected by our own thinking, whether positive or negative — and that thinking alters the reflection we see. If our thoughts are negative, our image can become distorted until it looks as grotesque as a reflection in a funny mirror at a carnival. That reflection is affected by our thinking habits; therefore the reflection of our self-image constantly changes as our current ideas about ourselves change.

You may be asking yourself right now, "What's so important about having a good self-image anyway?" It's important to have a good self-image because *your self-image sets the stage for your entire life,* and because God intended from the beginning for you to have a good image of yourself. This is why He made you in His *own* image. God has a wonderful self-image and He made *you* just like Himself!

From the very beginning God intended for man to be just like Him. The only problem is that the devil hates you and me and does not want us to know that we have the right to be just like God — *but we do have a right!*

God wants you to know *who you are in Him* so He can complete *His* work through you. For this to happen, you really must have a good image of yourself! If you have a poor self-image, it will cause you to pull your life around by your own power instead of driving your own life through Jesus Christ.

A good self-image will get you anywhere and everywhere God wants you to be. But if you don't have a good self-image, no matter where God wants you to go, you won't get there — because your self-image affects the way you present yourself, and the way others receive you. If you have a good self-image, you can present yourself positively, lovingly, and freely, and then that is the way people will see you. A positive, healthy self-image will provoke a positive, healthy response from others, reinforcing the good. On the other hand, a poor self-image will produce a poor response from others which will only reinforce your problem.

Some of the symptoms of a bad self-image are: feelings of unworthiness and of being undeserving of anything good, depression, lethargy, lack of initiative, insecurity, fear of people and the future, failure to maintain long-term relationships. (Now don't these symptoms sound as though they came straight from the devil? They did!)

But there *is* hope for anyone and everyone to have a good self-image — regardless of what he has been through in his life. It doesn't matter if you have been through a divorce, if you have been sexually abused, if you are overweight, if you are physically handicapped, or if you have a bad character trait of some kind. No matter what you feel is causing your bad self-image, it cannot stand in the way of your developing a good one *if* you see yourself as God sees you. And here is the image God has of you.

# God's Mirror Reflection

**God said, Let Us [Father, Son, and Holy Spirit] make mankind in Our image, after Our likeness; and let them have complete authority over the fish of the sea, the birds of the air, the [tame] beasts, and over all the earth, and over every thing that creeps upon the earth.**

**So God created man in His own image, in the image and likeness of God he created him; *male* and *female* He created them.**

**Genesis 1:26,27 AMP**

So your entire image should be based on the fact that God said, "Let Us (meaning God the Father, God the Son, and God the Holy Spirit) make man (male and female) in Our image." And when God looks in the mirror, because you are His image, He sees you. The more you walk with God, the more you see God when you look in the mirror. That is what He wants from us — not to look at our own weaknesses and what we cannot do, but to know that when He lives in us we can accomplish anything He can accomplish.

God expects us to have such a tremendous infilling of God the Father, God the Son, and God the Holy Spirit that when we look in the mirror we see God and He's so big in our lives that we can't see ourselves. We just see Him. When we look at it that way, we're centered in on the God in us and not on ourselves, and that makes the difference.

Very often I recommend to those whom I am helping to develop a good self-image that they stand in front of their mirror and say:

"I am a winner!

I am a child of Almighty God!

I am born to win!

I can do all things through Christ!

I am an overcomer!

I am a *be*-comer!"

Learn to see yourself as God sees you — saved, filled with the Spirit, healed, prosperous, and blessed. Now to be able to do that and believe it, you must believe that you *are* worth something — and that belief can only come from within you. The motivation *must* come from within. You're the only one who can convince yourself to work hard to be who and what you desire to be.

Why should you work so hard to keep a good self-image once you have it? Because the devil is constantly trying to steal it from you.

Now here is something that is very important for you to realize. The reason the devil works so hard against you and me is because he is mad at us. You see, all the devil ever wanted was to be like God. In fact, he wanted it so much that he got thrown out of heaven for setting himself up like God. Then God turned around and made man like Himself. Well, that just stung the devil, so he's been mad at man ever since. If he can do anything to put us down or hurt us or make us lower than him, he will do it. And the first place he is going to start is with our opinion of ourselves. He knows that if he can get us to think we are worthless, then we'll never be successful, and we will never be what God wants us to be.

The devil has robbed us of our self-image. He has stolen it right out of our minds. He has stolen what

God gave us for an image — God's image — because the devil knew that if he took it out of us, we wouldn't act like God. So he attacked our minds and said, "All right, I'm going to make them think that they're ugly. I'm going to make them think that they're not worth anything, that they can't overcome anything, even if they wanted to."

And by doing that he has caused many people to have a bad self-image and to lose their joy and strength!

How many times have you looked into a mirror and turned this way and that way, looking at different angles of your body, and the whole time thinking that you didn't like anything about yourself? I have watched the devil steal a God-given self-image from many men and women as they have twisted and turned looking in a mirror, because they didn't see God's image there.

You see, the devil is going to attack us in any way he can. His desire is to destroy our self-image and then ultimately to destroy our soul. That's why we should work hard to maintain a good self-image — so we can defeat the devil on a regular basis. And the way we do that is by keeping our self-image built up in a "God-image."

Unfortunately most people have a hard time believing that God loves us so much that He truly did give us His very own image. So we have to remind ourselves and have to correct ourselves. The next time you look in the mirror and start to say something like, "I'm ugly," just stop and say: "No, I'm not ugly. I'm made in the image of God, and He's certainly not ugly. He's God, and I'm made in His likeness and in His image; therefore, I must have something going for me."

Remind yourself of this and remember that you are God's mirror reflection. In fact, stop right now and go over to a mirror and say that last quote to yourself *out loud.*

*God likes looking at you*, because you are His image. You're important. You're righteous. You're worthy. But I can't convince you — only *you* can convince yourself.

When you believe that you are worth something, you can believe you can do anything with God in you **. . . because He Who lives in you is greater (mightier) than he who is in the world** (1 John 4:4 AMP), and you **. . . have strength for all things in Christ Who empowers . . .** you (Phil. 4:13 AMP).

Right now, just take a minute to center in on the Lord. Meditate on who you are in Christ. See yourself as God sees you — in His image, in His likeness. Realize that you are valuable and precious to Him!

Now you may be hesitating because you really don't know how to meditate on Jesus Christ, because maybe you don't know Who He is. You haven't personally met Him. If that's true for you, then before we go any farther, let me introduce Him to you, because without Him you can never achieve a good self-image. Don't let the devil run you around any longer. Don't let the devil steal your self-image from you any longer. Be the person God called you to be.

God loved you enough that He sent His only begotten Son to this earth to die for your sins so that you could have eternal life. (John 3:16.) Through our own self-righteousness we cannot earn the right to live with God in heaven for eternity because we have all sinned. But Jesus came to this earth and was tempted in *every* way that a person can be tempted, and He did *not* sin. Then He was crucified by mankind and became the sacrifice for our sins. So when we accept Him as our Savior, we can have eternal life with the Father through the righteousness of His Son, Jesus Christ.

To receive the Lord into your heart and life, just say this prayer out loud:

"Father, in the name of Jesus I come to You now. I realize that I have failed You and I haven't always been all You have called me to be. But, Lord, now I ask You to come into my heart. Forgive me now of all my sins and cleanse me of all unrighteousness. Fill me with Your Holy Spirit from the top of my head to the bottom of my feet.

"Take me one hundred percent — all of me. Use me and speak to me. Let me hear Your voice.

"Jesus, I accept You as my Lord and Savior. And when I ask with a believing heart, I know You accept me. I give You all the glory and all the praise. Amen."

Praise the Lord! You have just taken the most important step in getting a good self-image. But more importantly, you now have eternal life with God the Father in heaven! You have been born again in your spirit, and this new birth sets you free to become your best. You are free to be great. Don't be afraid to be great. David was an unknown shepherd boy who became a king. (1 Samuel 16.) You can do the same. Just let Jesus shine through you!

In Ephesians the Apostle Paul says that we are blessed with all scriptural blessings in Christ! You are royalty, and you are precious and valuable because you represent Jesus.

## What Others Think

Now one of the major ways the devil will try to make you forget that you are worthy is through the influence of other people and what they think about you. The problem with basing your self-image on what others think about you is that some people will think good of you and others will think bad of you. Your self-image must not be affected by anybody's opinion but your own. What's important is what you think — how you look at yourself — how you perceive yourself.

I have had many opportunities in my life to let what others think about me influence my self-image. When I was a little country girl in Mississippi and was crippled and had scars all over my face, my Sunday School teachers, many people in my community, and even my relatives told me: "You're not going to be healed. You've got to get this notion out of your head. God's not going to heal you, Honey. The doctors have said that you will never walk again." Now, understand that they thought they were helping me. They truly thought I needed to face reality, but I knew that *all I needed to face was truth!*

I said to myself, "I will not hear it. I will not receive it." I just smiled at them and was sweet to them. But I kept saying in my spirit, "I'm going to be healed. I'm going to walk again. I'm going to do what God called me to do."

It didn't matter that they thought I wasn't going to walk again. It didn't matter that they thought I was going to stay a cripple. What *they* thought about my life didn't matter. Only what *I* thought made any difference. You see?

We worry so much about what everybody else thinks, and it doesn't matter what they think. It doesn't change a thing. It doesn't get you a step farther and won't take you a step backward if you don't listen to them. But you have to know who you are in Christ, or they will be able to convince you and you will develop a bad self-image.

So what do you do? You don't get mad at them. You love them. You smile at them. You hug them and then you just tune them out. But you make sure you are in tune with the Lord and you make sure that *you listen to what He says.* You can't do that without His Word and without spending time with him. You must spend that time in fellowship with Him and begin to let Him feed you. Then let Him change you on the inside.

*Learn to see yourself as God sees you!*

What I think of me matters, but what others think of me really doesn't matter. Now that may seem a little harsh or self-centered, but you must realize that if your self-image is based on what people think of you, it will always be unstable — because sometimes people will applaud you and sometimes they will make you feel that you are a failure.

I learned that it doesn't matter what anybody else in the world thinks of Cheryl, because what they think won't make me and it won't break me. It won't make me a better person, and it won't make me a worse person. What anybody else thinks of me does not matter.

Now don't misunderstand me. I love for people to love me. But I realize that I can't make everybody love me. I have no control over what anybody else thinks of me. So what they think of me doesn't change me in any way. What I think of me affects my self-image, and that's why I must base it on what God thinks of me.

Of course, that's good because all the things God thinks of me and thinks of you are good. The Father loves us and thinks we are wonderful or else He wouldn't have entrusted us with Jesus. He wouldn't have entrusted us with the Holy Spirit. He wouldn't have entrusted us with the right to become the sons and daughters of God. He wouldn't have entrusted us with His righteousness. He wouldn't have entrusted us with the power to lay hands on the sick, to preach the gospel, to teach, and to cast out demons.

Obviously, the Father has quite a bit of faith in us. Now if we can get the same kind of faith in ourselves that God the Father has in us, we'll begin to see that we're pretty important. But until we realize how important we are and have a good self-image, we won't ever lay hands on the sick, or preach the gospel, or share the love of Jesus with others. We won't ever act like, walk like, or talk like the righteousness of God until we really believe that we have these rights and that we are important enough that God entrusted us with these beautiful things.

He trusts us because He knows how important we are. *You* may not know how important you are, but God does. And He entrusted you with His only Son Jesus. He gave Him to you because He knew you were worth giving Him to. You must realize that you are worthy to carry Jesus, to carry the Holy Spirit, to carry power, and to carry righteousness.

So what anybody else thinks of you doesn't change you. God obviously thinks you're wonderful, because in 3 John 2 He said that He wants you to be in health and to prosper. God wants you saved, healed, filled with the Holy Ghost, walking in victory, completed, and overcoming. He wants all these things for you.

Nothing can get you through tragedy, nothing can get you through the day, nothing can get you through your job, and nothing can get you through your family problems the way a good self-image can. The way you think of yourself is the most important factor in a victorious life.

When I lost all those pageants, my self-image wasn't based on whether I won or not. I could have let it be based on what people thought of me, but I *chose* differently. I chose to believe that my worth was based on what God thought of me, not what people thought. A good self-image must be based on the knowledge and understanding of who we are in Christ and Who Christ is in us.

*Who are we in Christ? New creatures* — **Therefore if any man be in Christ, he is a new creature: old things are passed away; behold, all things are become new** (2 Cor. 5:17); *His workmanship* — **For we are his workmanship, created in Christ Jesus unto good works, which God hath before ordained that we should walk in them** (Eph. 2:10); *His image* — **But we all, with open face beholding as in a glass the glory of the Lord, are changed into the same image from** glory to glory, even as by the Spirit of the Lord (2 Cor. 3:18).

*Who is Christ in us? The hope of glory* — **To whom God would make known what is the riches of the glory of this mystery among the Gentiles; which is Christ in you, the hope of glory** (Col. 1:27); *the life we live* — **I am crucified with Christ: nevertheless I live; yet not I, but Christ liveth in me: and the life which I now live in the flesh I live by the faith of the Son of God, who loved me, and gave himself for me** (Gal. 2:20); *wisdom, righteousness, sanctification, and redemption* — **But of him are ye in Christ Jesus, who of God is made unto us wisdom, and righteousness, and sanctification, and redemption** (1 Cor. 1:30).

This is the key. When God is in you, you can do anything, become anything, and overcome anything. But you must set this power free in you by believing that you *can*! You are either letting things happen to you or you are making things happen. And with a good self-image, you can determine your destiny.

Now one reason some people have a problem controlling their destiny is because they are continually comparing themselves with others. This is especially true for young people who gauge themselves by what their peers determine is acceptable, instead of measuring up to their own potential.

I learned this during my pageant years. The first couple of years I compared myself to the other girls. I never measured up, because someone else always won. They either looked better than I did, or they sang better than I did, or their clothes were prettier than mine, or they had something better than I had — every time. But over the years, I discovered that all the Lord ever expected of me was to be the best Cheryl I could be. And that is all I should ever expect of myself. When I got that into my head and then into my heart and began to practice it, it became not just a thought but a habit so that I did it automatically. Now I automatically compare myself to my own ability and to what I should be and what I am becoming. As you begin doing this, it will make a difference in your own self-image.

Now that we have an understanding of what a self-image is, let's take a look at *your* self-image — *who do you think you are?*

# 3
# Taking Charge of Your life

Of course, before you can take charge of your life and change your self-image, you must look inside yourself to find out *what your self-image is.* Proverbs 23:7 says that as a person thinks in his heart, so is he. So the best way to discover what your self-image is, is to find out what is in your heart. I have found that the best way to do that is to write down what you think of yourself. So at the end of this chapter I have provided you a worksheet for that purpose.

You will notice that it has a place for you to make two lists. First, you should list five characteristics about yourself that you do *not* like. Second, list five characteristics about yourself that you *do* like. And be sure to list both inside and outside attributes — emotional, mental, and spiritual, as well as physical.

Now, look at your lists and ask yourself these qustions:

1. How many of the characteristics that I listed were outside ones?

2. Which characteristics do I feel I *can* change?

3. Which characteristics do I feel I *cannot* change?

4. Which characteristics bother me?

5. Which characteristics bother me all the time?

If you are like most people, on your "do *not* like list" you probably listed more outside characteristics than inside ones. And many of these probably bother you almost all of the time, yet it is likely that you don't feel it is within your power to change them.

So at this point, I want to address those characteristics you feel you *cannot* change — the negatives — and show you how you *can* change those negatives into positives.

## Turning Negatives into Positives

For many people who read this book I could probably have more appropriately called this section "Turning Positives into Negatives," rather than turning negatives into positives. If that is your case, don't worry, you're not alone.

As I travel from city to city holding services and seminars, I usually ask people in my audiences to make their two lists, as you have just done. Almost without exception, the majority of them can immediately fill in the list of things they do *not* like about themselves, but have a very difficult time listing the things they do like. Most people know exactly what's wrong with themselves, but nothing that is right about them. And the reason for that is that many people have the tendency to *center on* or *spotlight* their bad characteristics. What they don't realize is that when they do that, it makes other people do the same thing. Being in beauty pageants helped me learn that principle real quick!

As I mentioned earlier, since I was very young I've had scars on my face as a result of that car accident. I also had crooked teeth and was upset about my looks most of the time. My parents never had enough money to get my teeth straightened, and there was nothing medically that could be done about the scars. Well, when I began entering pageants as God had called me to do, I tried my best to deal with those negative features. But then something happened that just made everything much worse!

I was traveling with a group of university singers called the Madrigals. We were on a weekend trip to Meridian, Mississippi, and Mobile, Alabama. We had just done two television tapings and were on our way home.

One of the guys in the group was feeling down in the dumps because his wallet had been stolen. Since I was always "Miss Cheer Up the World," I tried to help my friend feel better. As we stepped down off the bus, I jumped on his back and challenged him to carry me across the parking lot. Pretty soon, he was smiling a little, starting to get cheered up, and so he decided to spin around. Well, we both got dizzy and as he turned, he bent over. I did not have a good hold on him so I slid off his back and fell headlong onto the concrete, asphalt and gravel, landing with my full weight on my face. Because we had gotten up quite a bit of speed as we were turning, in a matter of seconds my face was mangled by the gravel.

I stood up with blood dripping down my face and felt with my tongue, only to find that my two front teeth were missing! There were only two little nubs where my own teeth had been.

It was dark and we searched in the gravel for my two teeth, but we couldn't find them. My mouth had already begun to swell. My lip and chin were torn up, as well as the side of my face. The cuts were not clean ones like those caused by the windshield when I was in that car wreck, but were jagged scrapes.

My first thoughts were, "Oh no, not again. Why me? I've had to overcome so much already. Why me?" Every negative emotion that could come from the devil flooded my mind — fear, doubt, anxiety. I felt that my quest for the title of Miss America was now surely over. I just wanted to forget it all. *I was tired of fighting.* Life was just too hard. (Haven't you felt that way before?)

Well, the leader of our group rushed me to the local hospital, and as I lay there in that emergency room, I thought to myself, "I've made the decision before, and I can make it again." And even though at that moment I had no desire to be happy or to overcome, I said, "God, You've got to help me one more time." Then I simply said, "I'll make it. I *will* make it." From that moment, it was not just a one-time decision but rather a minute-by-minute decision.

The medical staff did what they could for me at the hospital, cleaning the gravel from the wounds and placing stitches where needed, then we returned to the hotel. From there we had a six-hour bus ride home. My arm was in a sling because I had also dislocated my shoulder. I was in terrible pain. Every part of my face hurt. The exposed nerves where my teeth had been broken were very sensitive. I could hardly breathe, and eating was extremely difficult.

After we had arrived at the college, my roommate drove me home. I remember my mother's reaction when I walked into our house. She hugged me and began crying, saying that I looked worse than when I had been in the car wreck.

My sister Paulette took me to the dentist. With his help, and through a series of miracles, I was able to keep what remained of my two front teeth through what was then a new dental technique called "bonding." However, later on I discovered that even if I could get enough money to get braces to straighten all my crooked teeth, I couldn't wear them now that my teeth were permanently bonded. It would ruin the bonding if I did.

Now I was faced with the big decision: should I enter competition in the spring in spite of fresh scars and broken teeth? At first, I thought there was no way. Surely this was too big a situation for even God to turn around. Perhaps this was His way of telling me to stop.

But no, I had learned long ago that our loving Father never sends adversity to teach His children. God is a good God, and only good things can come from Him. And even the bad that the devil brings our way can be turned for our good by our heavenly Father. (James 1:17.) I realized that all the negative things that had happened to me were attacks of the enemy designed to stop me, or at least to slow me down.

Well, I decided that I couldn't change the facts (my crooked teeth and scarred face), so I decided that I would concentrate on the positive side of my appearance instead of the negative.

Well, you know the story of how many pageants I entered and lost time and time again. At that point I could have said, "That's it. I'm not doing this any more. I'm ugly because I've got crooked teeth and scars on my face, and I just can't win a pageant."

But I had learned that what I think of me not only affects my self-image, it also affects what other people think of me. When I don't notice that my teeth are crooked, other people don't notice either. When I smile, I know that people are looking at my smile, not at my teeth. When I don't notice my scars, others don't notice them either, because they're not looking at the lines on my face, they're looking at me, at my face as a whole.

So I knew that if I centered in on the negative, I would never be Miss America, but if I focused on the positive and kept a good self-image, I could become all that God wants me to become.

And it wasn't very long afterwards that I won the title of Miss America — with a scarred face and crooked teeth!

You see, if I had focused attention on all the negatives of my life, I would never have become Miss America. I would still be worrying over them and hating them and probably have a very bad self-image.

This is what you do with negative characteristics which cannot be changed to positive ones any other way. *You change them to positives by not focusing on them, but instead focusing on your heart.* You have a choice. You can dwell on the negatives and let them defeat you, or you can set them aside and forget them. I could not change or alter my crooked teeth or the scars on my face, but I could make the decision to forget them and keep on smiling!

I developed the inside of me so positively that no one noticed the outside. And the way I did that was by studying the Bible, by watching my confession (the words that came out of my mouth), and by developing my heart. When you do these things, you will see yourself in a new light, and so will others. Then you can start taking charge of your life and do what God wants you to do.

I'l give you an example. The roommate I had at Mississippi State University for four years was a precious girl who had the Holy Ghost and loved God with all her heart. She was born with no fingers on either hand except for her index finger and her thumb. Not only that, she had a club foot too — all from birth. Because we were best friends, I was with her all the time. But do you know that during those four years as roommates and during the two years I had known her before college, she never once mentioned her hands or her foot!

She could type 60 to 80 words a minute. She could play the piano. She could play tennis. She could do anything I could do, and usually better. And because she never centered in on the negative, I knew her six months before I noticed that she had a club foot and no fingers. *I didn't notice because she didn't notice.*

Finally one day her mother started talking to me about her daughter's problem and I wondered what she was talking about. Then it dawned on me, as she talked about her daughter's hands and foot, that I had missed something. But even after I found out about the daughter's problems, I didn't notice them, because she did not spotlight them.

So quit centering in on your faults. I guarantee you that if you are a Christian and you ask God what your bad points are, He won't be able to think of any. He won't be able to see any, because you are covered by the blood of Jesus. You need to begin to see yourself as God sees you.

Now many people have a problem with centering in on their positive attributes instead of their faults, because they think it's prideful and egotistical to do that. But there is a big difference between having a good self-image and being prideful. Many times in His Word the Lord reminds us to love our neighbor as ourselves. (Lev. 19:18,34; Matt. 19:19, 22:39; Rom. 13:9; Gal. 5:14; James 2:8.) Now if He expected us to hate ourselves, why would He have said for us to love our neighbor *as* ourselves?

Now here is a fact that may be hard to swallow, but it's true — no one is going to love you more, no one is going to protect you more, and no one is going to be more concerned about you than you yourself. But see, that's not wrong, as long as your thinking is right — as long as you're striving to be the best you can be so you can accomplish all that God has put you here on earth to accomplish for His glory.

You've got to be able to understand this principle, and you've got to be able to stand up for it, because there are a lot of people who will try to lay a heavy "spiritual trip" on you by telling you that you're wrong, that you're just looking at yourself. But remember, God made you in His image, and He expects you to love that image. In fact, it hurts Him greatly when you reject that image and don't do what you should be doing to discipline yourself and take care of it.

## Goal-Setting/Discipline

At the risk of causing you to close this book, put it down, and never pick it up again, I am going to give you some tips on goal-setting and discipline — the most despised words in the English language!

It's at this point that most people say, "Yeah, it all sounded good up till now. But forget talking to me about setting goals and being disciplined. I've tried all those nice-sounding things, and I just can't do them. I start out okay, then life just seems to overtake me and I'm right back where I started."

Well, if that is what you are thinking, the reason I can read your thoughts is because I've been in your place before. Believe me, I didn't just walk out on the stage after five years of being in pageants and win the Miss America title without first having *learned* how to set my goals, then to be disciplined enough to achieve them. You must *learn* how to set goals. Then once you've learned how to do that, you must set your will to do whatever God asks you to do in order to reach those goals.

In order to be a goal-setter and a disciplined person, you must know who you are in Christ Jesus — remember the example of looking in the mirror? In other words, you must believe you are worth the effort it's going to take to set your goals and to be disciplined enough to achieve them. And, believe me, you will experience the benefits of a strong good self-image and success in your life once you set goals and become disciplined.

Many people are not successful in these two areas because they don't let their joy lead them through every day of their lives. In a later chapter I will share with you the greatest secret God has ever revealed to me — how to *always* be happy. But right now let me show you the way to set your goals and be disciplined so you can accomplish whatever God wants you to accomplish, and therefore be totally fulfilled in your life through having a good self-image — as He intends for you.

*A dream* — that's what your goals start with — a dream. Then once you have a dream, you set goals to see that dream become reality. The dream of being Miss America was in my heart before I ever graduated from high school, but reality was still a long way off. I had to make my dream a goal; then once I did that, I had to work and be disciplined to see the dream come true.

I didn't start with the Miss America title as my immediate goal or I would have gotten discouraged — you see, I spent five years preparing to be what I had dreamed I could be someday! Let me show you what I mean — here is what happened to me in the years after the dream to become Miss America was birthed in my heart:

| | |
|---|---|
| 1976 First Year: | Won First Runner-Up in Local Pageant |
| 1977 Second Year: | Won Second Runner-Up in Local Pageant |
| 1978 Third Year: | Won Third Runner-Up in Local Pageant (by this time things looked bleak) |
| 1979 Fourth Year: | Won Local Pageant for First Time Won First Runner-Up in Miss Mississippi Pageant |

1980 Fifth Year:      Won Local Pageant for Second Time
Won Miss Mississippi Pageant
Won Miss America Pageant

During those years of losing, I *chose* to *learn* from what seemed to be failure by turning it into a positive experience and working even harder to prepare for the next pageant. I refused to compare myself with anyone else, working only toward the goal I had chosen for myself. It's important that you set your own goals and not let someone else set them for you; otherwise, during the tough times you'll crumble and so will your goals, because your heart will not be set on achieving them. Taking on someone else's goals can be devastating — especially to your self-image. Be comfortable with your own goals.

Now notice that I did not set just one big goal of becoming Miss America, and then go after it. That would have worn me down after all those years of not reaching my final goal. Instead I set short-range, intermediate, and long-range goals and kept my eyes on accomplishing each goal along the way.

For instance, my short-range goal was to learn how to prepare myself to be the very best pageant contestant I could possibly be. You remember how I went into my first local contest, the Miss Choctaw County Pageant, without any preparation — and lost? Well, from that experience I learned that preparation is vitally important to winning, as is true for anything worth doing in life. Short-range goals are for our own self-confidence. We need to see results in a short amount of time in order to keep moving onward and upward.

Then intermediate goals keep us from getting discouraged and quitting. My intermediate goals were to win preliminary pageants. And as I reached those goals, it gave me a sense of accomplishment, which was important to me to keep me working toward my long-range goal, which was to win the Miss America title. It's the long-range goal that keeps us looking up and trusting God to take us much farther than we can even imagine.

It's important that you not be afraid to set goals. To have no goals is to be without any direction in life. If you have no destination in mind, you will never know when you have arrived! If you need to adjust your goals along the way, do it, but at least set them. And I believe the best way for you to do that is to write them down. This helps you to establish in your mind that you are serious about striving to reach your goals.

Now don't let it intimidate you to write down your goals. That's not the purpose of goal-setting. No one is going to hold those goals over your head until every one of them is reached. Writing down your goals simply initiates action — it gets you off your seat and on your feet!

Right now you can turn to the back of this chapter and see your Goal-Setting Worksheet. This worksheet is provided to help you write down your short-range, intermediate, and long-range goals. Keep in mind that goals can be any kind — physical, academic, financial, spiritual, social, material, etc. I've provided you with a few examples to help you get started. First write your own goals. Then as you reach the goals you've written down, you can go back and mark them out. When you do, you will feel from the top of your head to the soles of your feet the tremendous sense of accomplishment that comes as you achieve a good self-image!

What I am saying to you is, *dare to dream* — then turn your dreams into reality! Don't be discouraged when time seems to drag by. Make it work to your advantage by giving you the optimum opportunity to become fully prepared. This is the place where most people give up on their goals — when it comes to *discipline*. That word seems to spell misery and failure to many people, but that's because they misunderstand what discipline really is.

You see, discipline is *making* things happen, rather than *letting* them happen. When I am disciplined, I am in control. When I'm not disciplined, I'm out of control. But discipline can only come through willingness and obedience to God. *Willingness and obedience will cause you to become disciplined over a period of time* — because discipline takes time to develop.

You begin by focusing on what you do best, then setting goals, then working to reach those goals in order to fulfill the dream you have in your heart for that area of your life. You have got to decide once and for all who is in charge of your life — and who is going to take authority in your life!

First your *dream* becomes a *goal*, then your goal becomes a *work*, then your work becomes a *discipline*. But the *reward* of that discipline is tremendous!

When I was five years old I sat down at our old piano one night and just began playing without having had any lessons. My mama and daddy instantly knew that my musical ability was a special gift from God.

Well, as I got older, I learned gospel tunes by just listening to them and playing them over and over at our house. Music was a big part of my family's life. Everyone would gather around the piano after supper and we would all sing gospel hymns and clap our hands in time with the music. Those were very special times for us all, and I felt very comfortable in that environment.

Then just before I entered the third grade, the time finally came when I was able to take "real" piano lessons. Mama and Daddy had worked hard to scrape together the six dollars and fifty cents it took to enable me to take lessons from our school's music teacher. Little did I know how much that experience would affect my life, for it was from this young country teacher, Becky Curtis, that I learned to set goals and then discipline myself to reach them.

Becky's motto was: "Always have a goal, and once you've reached it, set another. And remember, no matter how good you get, never be satisfied. Never! Because once you're satisfied, you have nowhere to go but down. If you're always striving to reach a new goal, you're certain to grow."

It all became real to me when I first began taking lessons from Becky. There were few things in life I could do well, but playing the piano was one of them, so it was important to me to succeed at my lessons. I wanted to impress her during my first lesson, so I played the most complicated piece of gospel music I knew. She seemed impressed, but then opened a book called the *John Thompson Songbook for Beginners*, put it on the piano, and asked me to play a piece from it. My pride just crumbled. I knew I couldn't play that music because I couldn't read it — I only knew how to play by ear.

But then I was sparked with an idea. Very innocently I asked Becky to play it first, knowing that she had no idea that all I had to do was hear the tune once and I would be able to play it fairly well — as though I was reading the music for the first time.

Lesson after lesson I did this until finally the day came when Becky refused to play a new piece first. I knew my charade had come to an end and I began to cry. In my heart I wanted Becky to be impressed with me more than I wanted anything else, but now I was sure she was disappointed in me.

I'll never forget what happened that life-changing day. After wrapping her arm around me and consoling me and telling me how wonderful it was that I could play by ear, Becky began to show me that there was a whole new world of music out there just waiting for me to explore, if I would set my goals, then be disciplined enough to accomplish them.

Then she gave me a taste of what I had been missing. She played all kinds of music — classical, pop, country, jazz. I did not even realize then what an important role this experience would play in the realization of my dream — for music was my talent competition that helped me win the Miss America title years later — all because I set my goals and was disciplined enough to accomplish them — and because I didn't get discouraged enough to quit during those long years of working toward that goal.

## Thinking, Speaking and Acting

Now this is important. There's only one way for you to make what happened to me happen to you. And that is by changing your habits of thinking, speaking and acting. And that requires daily discipline.

It all boils down to paying attention to what you think, say, and do on a *daily* basis — that's the key.

The first thing you must do is to concentrate on changing your negative thoughts into positive ones. When you begin to slip back into old habits of feeling negative and down on yourself, nip those feelings in the bud — *immediately*. The minute you feel the negative thoughts begin to rise up in your mind, put your discipline into action and stop your mind from being ruled by those negative impressions. Don't entertain those thoughts at all — not even the tiniest bit — because if you do, they'll get a foothold in your mind. Once they do that, it's downhill from there.

In 2 Corinthians 10:5 the Apostle Paul speaks of **casting down imaginations, and every high thing that exalteth itself against the knowledge of God, and bringing into captivity every thought to the obedience of Christ.**

The primary way to control your thoughts is by controlling what you put into your mind. If you are continually watching television and putting your mind into neutral instead of reading the Word of God which puts your mind into drive, you will not be able to control your thoughts. It is our human nature to be negative, but salvation or the New Birth brought God's nature into us, which is entirely positive. The new man within you desires to excel and has the ability to do so, but you must let him!

In Romans 12:2 in *The Amplified Bible,* Paul says, **Do not be conformed to this world — this age, fashioned after and adapted to its external, superficial customs. But be transformed (changed) by the [entire] renewal of your mind — by its new ideals and its *new attitude* — so that you may prove [for yourselves] what is the good and acceptable and perfect will of God, even the thing which is good and acceptable and perfect [in His sight for you].**

Your mind is the battleground. (2 Cor. 11:3.) It is there that the battle with Satan is either won or lost. You must renew your mind to the fact of your worth to God as His child and to the reality of Who Jesus is inside you.

Make a quality decision to control your thoughts, **. . . bringing every thought into captivity to the obedience of Christ** (2 Cor. 10:5). A sound mind is a disciplined mind. (2 Tim. 1:7.)

The next thing you must discipline is your speaking. There is great power in what we say. If we are continually repeating negative things about ourselves, we will see negative results and behavior in our lives. But if we "confess" positive things, we will see positive results and actions. You can talk yourself into a bad self-image, or you can talk yourself into a good self-image:

> **. . . For out of the fullness — the overflow, the superabundance — of the heart the mouth speaks.**
>
> **The good man from his inner good treasure flings forth good things, and the evil man out of his inner evil storehouse flings forth evil things.**
>
> **Matthew 12:34,35** AMP

> **Death and life are in the power of the tongue, and they who indulge it shall eat the fruit of it [for death or life].**
>
> **Proverbs 18:21** AMP

You can speak life to your good self-image and death to your bad self-image. It's up to us to set the tone of our lives by the words that come out of our mouths, for the words that come out of our mouths are formed by the thoughts that are in our minds. I've seen people's lives destroyed just by the way they thought and talked. You can be physically disciplined all you want to, but if you do not discipline your thoughts and words, you will tremendously influence your self-image negatively.

*Choose* to feel good about yourself. Say good things about yourself every morning. I have every opportunity to be down, just as you do, but I don't choose to do so. It does absolutely no good to be defeated, so why waste your time?

*Smile* and control your thoughts and words. (Phil. 4:6-8.) Then help others to feel good about themselves. Build them up by telling them good things out of the Word of God. When you focus on their good and teach them how to have a positive self-image, you get stronger and so do they.

Start every day with positive thoughts and words. Use confessions like these from the scriptures:

*"I let no corrupt communication proceed out of my mouth, but that which is good to edifying, that it may minister grace to the hearer. I grieve not the Holy Spirit of God, whereby I am sealed unto the day of redemption."* (Eph. 4:29,30.)

*"God is on my side. God is in me now. Who can be against me? He has given me all things that pertain unto life and godliness. Therefore, I am a partaker of His divine nature."* (2 Cor. 6:16; Rom. 8:31; John 10:10; 2 Peter. 1:3,4.)

*"I am a believer, and these signs follow me. In the name of Jesus, I cast out demons, I speak with tongues, I lay hands on the sick, and they recover."* (Mark 17:17,18.)

*"Jesus gave me authority to use His name. That which I bind on earth is bound in heaven, and that which I loose on earth is loosed in heaven. Therefore, in the name of the Lord Jesus Christ, I bind the principalities, the powers, the rulers of the darkness of this world. In the name of Jesus, I bind and cast down spiritual wickedness in high places and render them harmless and ineffective against me."* (John 16:23,24; Matt. 16:19; Eph. 6:12.)

*"I let the peace of God rule in my heart, and I refuse to worry about anything."* (Col. 3:15.)

Now once you begin thinking and talking positively, you must begin *acting* that way. Even as a child, I had an inner desire to become Miss America, but desire alone did not make that dream come true. When I was crippled in that tragic car accident and told by so many people that I would never walk again, I didn't accept my circumstances as the final authority in my life. I set my goal to be healed. Then I was disciplined and read the Word of God and prayed, which helped me to keep positive thoughts in my mind and positive words in my mouth. I controlled my attitude and refused bitterness. Then when my healing came, I did something with my opportunity!

The motivation must come from *you*! To get your actions in line for a good self-image, begin to practice all the things you know will make you a better person. Take anything in your life that you consider to be a negative action and begin to work on that area, turning it little by little into a positive action. And you must not get impatient, but maintain a positive attitude in spite of circumstances. You did not form your negative thinking habit in one day, and it will take more than one day to get into a positive thinking habit.

In Philippians 4:11 the Apostle Paul says, . . . **for I have learned, in whatsoever state I am, therewith to be** *content.* This does not mean that you should stop having drive and ambition, goals and visions, but it does mean that you should try not to feel sorry for yourself and complain when you think you should be farther along. *The Twentieth Century New Testament* translation of this verse reads, . . . **to be** *independent of circumstances* . . . .[1] But you can only do this as you discipline your thoughts, words, and actions through the Word of God.

God's Word builds a positive, healthy self-image because it mirrors Christ. When you stand on the strength of the Word, it takes the focal point off of *your* strength. Second Corinthians 3:18 says, . . . **beholding as in a glass the glory of the Lord,** (we) **are** *changed* into the same image from glory to glory, even as by the Spirit of the Lord.

If you are weak spiritually, set a goal to discipline yourself to pray and read the Bible.

If you are overweight, study nutrition, and get on a diet and exercise plan.

---

[1] *The 20th Century New Testament: Part II* (Tulsa: Spirit to Spirit Publications, Tulsa Christian Center, 1981).

If your grades are low, put yourself on a study program and surround yourself with people who are achievers.

If you need to be motivated, outline some goals for yourself and begin to plan for the future.

As you learn to control your *thoughts*, your *tongue*, and your *actions*, you can truly have a good self-image and in turn you will feel your very best about yourself.

You will *learn* to be the *best* you can be, and will therefore learn to take charge of your life. You may not always start out as a winner, but winning must begin somewhere in your life. And it begins with a dream in your heart. A dreaming machine is inside you — so dream and don't be afraid of your dreams. Find some "dream space" — some time and place in which you can be all by yourself to just imagine all the wonderful things that you can do and be! Then take those dreams and turn them into a gold mine of realistic goals.

"If you can dream it, you can become it . . . ." (Emerson).

# Worksheet A
# Self-Image Worksheet

## CHARACTERISTICS I DO *NOT* LIKE ABOUT MYSELF:

1.

2.

3.

4.

5.

## CHARACTERISTICS I *DO* LIKE ABOUT MYSELF:

1.

2.

3.

4.

5.

# Worksheet B
# Setting Goals

LONG-RANGE GOALS — My Dreams:

Examples: 1. To become Miss America.

2. To get in shape and become healthy.

**Goal**                          **Date Accomplished**

1.

2.

3.

4.

5.

## Worksheet B

### Page 2

INTERMEDIATE GOALS — The steps I am going to take to reach my long-range goals.

Examples: 1. Win local pageants.
2. Begin incorporating more fruit and vegetables into my diet one meal at a time. Then begin eating a little less at each meal. Go on an exercise program and stick to it; confess and meditate on scriptures.

1.

2.

3.

4.

5.

## Worksheet B

## Page 3

SHORT-RANGE GOALS — How I am going to prepare to get where I want to be:

Examples: 1. Learn how to fix my hair, wear makeup, walk properly; study Mississippi history and current events, etc.

2. Learn how to exercise by buying a good aerobics video like *Take Charge of Your Life with Cheryl & Friends* and a good exercise video like *Get Ready with Cheryl & Friends*; learn about nutrition and what is happening to my body when I eat what I'm presently eating.

1.

2.

3.

4.

5.

# 4
# Blaming Our Childhood

Whatever self-image we have, we developed it by *learning* it. Now that may not seem like an important point, but it is one of the most important, and here's why: because our self-image is learned, we can "unlearn" a negative one and *relearn* a positive one. In other words, if you have a bad self-image, you're not stuck with it!

Psychologists agree that our sense of self-worth is determined at a very early age. Some say that even by birth an infant knows whether or not he is loved and wanted. Certainly by pre-school age we all have a pretty good idea of what we think of ourselves.

My heart has been broken as I have traveled to churches all over America and seen childen who obviously do not feel good about themselves. And these are sometimes the ones who demand the most attention from their parents, just as I demanded a lot of attention at home in my own way in what was an unconscious cry for self-love and understanding.

Many times when parents correct their children wrongly, they do so because they truly believe they are helping them. The problem in the child's self-image comes as a result of how he *receives* that correction. The innocent and well-meaning act of correcting a child can lay the foundation in the mind of the child for a poor feeling about himself. His feelings can become the *neurotic basis of all his actions.*

And if he allows them to do so, these feelings can rule his adult life as well. Therefore a child can develop a terrible self-image and *blame it all on his childhood!* But see, negative childhood experiences are no excuse for a lack of self-esteem, because in the end we are all responsible for our *own* self-image, no matter what has happened to us. Even if we've been abused verbally, physically, sexually, mentally, or emotionally, we're still responsible for our own attitudes and actions. We're the ones who have to determine and live with our own self-image.

## "Unlearning" a Bad Self-Image

There are usually two basic responses to abuse (or at least an unhappy childhood) which cause a bad self-image.

One way that many people respond is by becoming over-achievers. They turn outward. They can't seem to ever get enough approval. But, as Christians, the need for the approval of others should not be the driving force with us. The only thing that should ever drive us is the name of Jesus and the desire to fulfill His perfect will in our lives. Love of the Lord is the only driving force that can help us to develop a truly lasting and good self-image.

In Philippians 3:14, Paul says that we need to press toward the mark. We need to run till the race is over. The one thing that should drive us to reach the mark, to finish the race, to fight a good fight of faith is a desire to please Jesus — not to be an overachiever for Jesus, but simply to please Him.

Pleasing the Lord takes two things: obedience and willingness. He doesn't need us to be the best. He doesn't need us to be the greatest. He doesn't need us to be better than anybody else. He just needs us to be obedient to His Word. And He needs our willing heart to accomplish what He puts within us to accomplish. Not what our mind can dig up or what the devil will try to push us to do, but what He tells us to do through His voice and His Word.

Now, concerning the second way people respond to their negative childhood experiences: many withdraw and turn inside themselves. This usually makes them negative and depressed. Many times, they become overweight as a result.

Recently when I was ministering on this subject to a group of women in a large church in California, a woman who was overweight came up to me after the meeting and told me that she had been abused as a child. She asked me if I believed she had gained weight as a reaction to having been abused. I would like for you to hear what I told her and reach out and take hold of it for your own life.

"Yes," I said, "I do believe that. But the devil will use those feelings as a 'cop out' to give you an excuse in your mind to stay overweight. That is a lie and a deception of the devil. You do not have to stay the way you are now.

"In the name of Jesus, you can tell the devil that he cannot hold that experience over you any more. In the name of Jesus, you can put it under your feet. You can lose that weight. You can get into shape. You can take charge of your life and overcome anything in it that you don't like — no matter what it is or what caused it."

The same is true for you. After you recognize what the cause of your problem really is (whatever may have happened to you in your childhood), then you should realize that your weight gain (or whatever is wrong with you) is only the *evidence* of the problem. You must then call down the problem and spiritually put it under your feet. When you do that, the evidence of the problem must come down with it.

So weight gain can no longer be an excuse. You can't blame it on the abuse you may have received back in your childhood, once you recognize that the abuse was sent by the devil. So, in the name of Jesus, that weight gain must go. You make that happen by taking control of your own life. And you do that by turning over control of your life to the Lord and by "calling those things that be not as though they were." (Rom. 4:17.)

In the name of Jesus, you don't have to stay overweight. You don't have to have a long face and a negative outlook. You can choose to be happy. You can choose to be thin. You can choose to take responsibility for your own life.

You cannot keep on *blaming your childhood* for your bad self-image. If you don't like yourself, don't stay that way! Set your will that *with God's help* YOU are going to change your self-image.

To "unlearn" a negative self-image, you must shake off all the wrong concepts and ideas that you have adopted for yourself which are contrary to what the Word of God says about you. To create a good self-image is to begin to see yourself as God sees you —

worthy, righteous, holy, pure, blameless, and Christlike. Remember, we are made in His image. (Gen. 1:26,27.)

Changing your mind about yourself can be one of the *most difficult things* that you'll ever do. After all, you've taken years to formulate what you think about yourself, and such a precious opinion as yours is not easily set aside. It can be done, however, with desire and determination — if you first *believe* that you can do it. If you never honestly believe that through the Word of God you *can change*, you will very likely spend the rest of your life wrestling with the frustrations of a bad self-image.

Believe that you have *within* yourself, *through* the Word and the power of God, the ability to get rid of all self-defeating thoughts and ideas about yourself. It won't happen overnight, believe me. Creating a good self-image where a negative one has existed for so long is not easy. It is a process of ridding yourself of things that seem to be as much a part of you as your name. It's choosing to see yourself as Christ sees you, taking the Word of God as the final authority — no matter what *you have learned to think and feel about yourself.*

It may take a long time for you to shake off some of the negative self-concepts that have attached themselves to you when you were a child. In fact, many times you'll find yourself unconsciously thrown backwards into your old thought patterns. When you recognize this happening, stop and remind yourself that this behavior is unhealthy, harmful, and self-defeating.

## Capitalize on the Good

I encourage you to capitalize on and take advantage of the good things that happened to you as a child.

My Aunt Dorothy has always been an inspiration in my life, which has helped to carry me through a lot of situations I don't know how I could have gotten through otherwise. She was my "builder-upper" in my childhood.

It was Aunt Dot who gave me my first "store bought" clothes. All my other clothes where made by Mama because we couldn't afford to buy "ready made" clothes from a store. I'll never forget when Aunt Dot gave me the little light-blue culottes and blue-striped shirt ensemble. I was so proud that I had something with a store tag on it.

Aunt Dot made an impression on me because she always looked nice. She wasn't wealthy by any means, but she took care of herself — always had her makeup on just right and her hair done nicely. And she was always sweet to everyone. I don't care if it was the worst-looking person on earth — she was always loving and kind to him, smiling.

I always thought, "When I grow up, I'm going to look like Aunt Dot; I'm going to act like her." She made me realize that it doesn't matter where you come from, you can be all that you want to be; it all depends on what you decide to do and how you act toward other people. Because of her inspiration, I made a decison early in life to be nice to *everybody* because every person I meet may be going through something difficult in his life and what I say and do may be the only thing that helps him overcome the problems he is facing that day.

So many people can't "see" other people and their needs because they are concentrating on the negative things in their own lives and wallowing in a bad self-image. Negativism and self-pity are harmful emotions. When the Word of God tells us to bring every thought into captivity and make it obedient to Christ (2 Cor. 10:5), it means for us to do the same with our emotions.

When you begin to think of how someone treated you during your childhood and you start to get into self-pity, which only produces a bad self-image, at that moment bind that emotion with the power in the name of Jesus. Let it have no part in you — for self-pity is the fruit of unforgiveness, and it will bind you in chains preventing you from having a good self-image. Just turn those emotions over to God — speak to the mountain of negativism and self-pity and say to it, "Be thou removed, and be thou cast into the sea." If you believe that what you say will happen, it will come to pass. (Mark 11:23.)

Yes, God calls us to wholeness and forgiveness, and we must not only recognize when we have harmful emotions, but we must also bind them. And this comes through studying the Word of God. For you see, Satan would like to use those harmful emotions to bind us in chains to keep us from having a good self-image and being effective witnesses for Christ. If we hold onto those negative emotions, reliving past hurts and thoughts, a root of bitterness will grow in us instead of a root of forgiveness. Hate and unforgiveness open to Satan the door of torment, while love and forgiveness open the door to Jesus and abundant living.

Believe that through the resurrection power of Jesus Christ your emotional bondage can be broken. And that is true for those who feel they had a bad childhood *and* for those *parents* who feel they have caused bad self-images in their children.

## What About the Parents?

Here I would like to say a word to parents who feel they may have caused their children's bad self-image.

If you are a parent, as you read this book you may begin to come under condemnation or feel guilty because you know you've done a lot of things that have caused your child the trauma that he has gone through in later life because of the wrong choices that you made while rearing him. If so, you must understand what is happening so you won't let it ruin your own self-image and so you can help your child now.

Many things have changed in child-rearing since I was young. We're a generation that faces the facts and the truth. Today we call things the way we see them. Sometimes that causes a lot of hurt because we're not a generation to hide from reality but one which faces it.

Maybe your child is very obese, or moody, or withdrawn, or an overachiever. You may have begun to think, "Well, maybe my child feels that he is abused." Or worse than that, it may be that your child has sought counseling or has even come right out and said that he feels abused — and you don't know what it is that you are supposed to have done wrong.

Well, the fact is that a generation ago parents were not aware that the negative things they planted in their children would come out the way they have in this generation. They did the best they could with the knowledge they had at the time. If you are one of those parents, the one thing I don't want you to get into while reading this book is self-condemnation or guilt. I want you to feel forgiveness — to know that even if you have failed your child you can receive forgiveness for that failure and get a clean slate and a new start with the Lord.

I realize that parents have to discipline their children. I am a very strict disciplinarian myself as a parent. And yet there is a way to discipline with positive correction, rather than saying something negative like, "You are an idiot," or, "You're stupid," or, "You can't do anything right." Those are the types of statements that can really sow seeds of a bad self-image in kids. And even though sometimes those words slip out of our mouths, we just need to remember to pray, "Lord, forgive me for saying that. I curse that bad seed which I may have planted in my child. I ask You, Father, to kill that negative thought in his mind and let me reinforce with positive correction so much that he won't remember the negative thing I said about him."

I believe that most times parents do the best they can. Of course, there are a few exceptions, a few parents who are really mean or cruel. But, as a whole, I think most parents do what *they think* is best at the time. Sometimes the devil has them confused into thinking that what they are doing is the best thing for the child, when in reality it is harmful. They have been deceived by Satan into believing that their harsh action is the best thing for the child — that it will save him heartache later on in life. It's their way of protecting and/or teaching their child.

Of course, such parents are often totally wrong, totally misled, and totally confused. Now listen — in times past God has allowed us a certain grace period during which our lack of knowledge has been covered by His mercy. This was done to allow healing to flow out to and through us. But now in these last days the Lord is granting us more knowledge and revelation of His Word for rearing our children and for the development of our own self-image. Therefore we are not going to be able to depend on God's grace as much as we did in the past.

The fact that today so-called good, godly, church-going people abuse their children sexually and otherwise is coming out into the open. No longer can we Christians hide behind our fear of facing the truth about our own faults and failures. The truth is coming out and believers must clean up their own acts and become accountable for their own actions.

The one thing you must do if you are a parent is to focus on the fact that there are such things as bad actions on the part of parents which can and do reinforce bad habits and attitudes in their children.

When your child does wrong, rather than scolding him harshly and calling him names, you might simply say, "That was not the right choice. You chose incorrectly in that action. That was not the right thing to do." But don't say, "You're a bad boy, you're a bad girl." Also never say, "You're a good boy, you're a good girl." Because that says to the child that there are times when he or she is not a good boy or a good girl.

As silly as it may seem, relating a child's actions to his character instills and reinforces in him the idea that if he does something bad, that means that he *is* bad, and if he does something good, that means he *is* good. Many times when my son does something good, I catch myself saying to him, "What a good boy you are." Whenever I hear myself saying that, I always try to remember to add, "But of course, you are *always* a good boy."

The devil would have us believe that we're bad seed and not good seed. We've got to believe and know that we are good seed, not bad seed, and that the devil does not have control over our lives. We might make incorrect decisions and have to pay the consequences of those wrong actions, but our wrong choices do not make us bad children or bad parents.

Parents need to be very, very careful with children, because most children desperately want their parents' approval. They desperately need to hear that they're loved — that even if they don't chose what their parents would have chosen for them, they are still loved and accepted. They need to feel that God still loves them and cares for them, so they will still have the opportunity to develop and maintain a good self-image.

You know, there is a lot of truth to the old saying, "You rear as you were reared." Now for those adults who were reared poorly and are now beginning to have children of their own, I would say this: You need to know that you can stop the pattern of incorrect rearing right here.

You can say, "No longer, devil, will this pattern continue from generation to generation. I will begin afresh and anew. This newness created between me as a parent and my child will establish a new pattern of correct, godly rearing with positive reinforcement and positive approval. Knowing that he has my approval, my child will know that he also has God's approval of him as a person, if not of his actions. He will learn that he doesn't have to do things to win my approval or my love. He has them just because he is who he is. That's all that matters. No longer will the old pattern continue. In the name of Jesus, I stop it. I call it null and void. It will not continue. It will not go forth. It will not go on from generation to generation. From this point on, it is stopped. No longer will it continue in this family."

Now by doing that, God's way, God's choice, God's purpose, and God's will for your children and for generations to come will continue in your family.

Now, it's true that you must discipline children. (Prov. 13:24.) Don't spare the rod and don't spoil the child. But you should only discipline in proper love and in proper timing, and only when it is necessary — not when you are angry or frustrated. Only discipline when the child needs to receive it, not when you need to give it.

Another important thing is to make sure that the devil understands that your tongue is under subjection to the Holy Spirit Who lives within you. And your tongue will only speak good things to your children. It will reinforce the positive in your children. It will cause to cease the negative things that the devil tries to plant in your children. Claim your children as good seed which is rooted in good soil. Declare that they will grow up strong and clean and will bring forth much fruit for Jesus Christ. Declare boldly that the devil can do nothing to stop your children and the generations after them from producing a good harvest.

Praying that type of prayer will help protect you from doing things that may cause you and your children to suffer from a bad self-image.

In Isaiah 54:13, the Lord says: **And all thy children shall be taught of the Lord; and great shall be the peace of thy children.** In *The Amplified Bible* this verse reads: **. . . and great shall be the peace and undisturbed composure of your children.**

That's a positive way to pray over your children. You can claim those scriptures and believe them for your children. Even if they have left home, you can still pray that over them in faith and God can change what your wrong words and actions in the past may have caused.

You can also use the scripture in Isaiah 58 as a prayer guide for your children. *The Living Bible* version of verses 9,10 reads:

> **Then, when you call, the Lord will answer, "Yes, I am here," he will quickly reply. All you need to do is stop oppressing the weak, and to stop making false accusations and spreading vicious rumors.**
>
> **Feed the hungry! Help those in trouble. Then your light will shine out from the darkness, and the darkness around you shall be as bright as day.**

God just wants us to know that not only is He listening to and answering our prayers, He expects us to *do* something. (God always wants us *to do* something). He needs us to cleanse ourselves, starting with our actions towards others! In other words, if we will just watch over our own mouths, minds, thoughts, bodies, souls, and spirits, then we will find we have much less time to be judgmental and critical of others. Then by cleaning up our own act, our light will be so bright and cheery it will literally chase away the darkness in our lives.

## Blaming Our Childhood

Remember, for the first and most vital years of his life, parents play an important role in helping the child form his self-image. If the parents consistently show love and affection, the child is more prone to see himself as worthy of being loved by others, by God, and even by himself. If there is a lack of emotional warmth and support from his parents, the child is likely to grow up doubting his lovableness and lacking self-acceptance.

There are some people who have suffered from a lack of support, but there are also some who have been abused in some way, and the effects of that abuse may have been devastating upon their self-image.

I want to say to you today that if your self-image has been distorted by such a blow as this, or if you are a parent who has been the abuser, beginning right now you can rise up and change that image. You can build a new, strong, good self-image by going over and over the scriptures and thoughts God has given you in this chapter.

Early in my life, I learned to be strong and to be the type of person who stood up for herself. That is where I began to form the attitude: "I am somebody and I am worth something, and no matter what obstacles come into my life, I don't have to do anything or conform to anything; I only conform to the Lord."

And you must say the same thing to yourself, and believe it.

Once we understand that we have received the Spirit and nature of Christ, we can then move on to developing our personalities in Him; or rather, His personality in us. It is the work of the Holy Spirit, as recorded in John 14:26, to reveal in us the attributes of Christ: **But the Comforter, which is the Holy Ghost, whom the Father will send in my name, he shall teach you all things, and bring all things to your remembrance, whatsoever I have said unto you.**

Jesus came to reveal the Father, but the Spirit came to reveal Jesus. I like what Paul says in 1 Corinthians 2:12: **Now we have received, not the spirit of the world, but the spirit which is of God; that we might know the things that are freely given to us of God.** God wants to reveal the nature of Christ within us. In allowing Him to reveal, by His Holy Spirit, the nature and personality of Christ in us, a positive self-image will be created. How much better could you feel about yourself than to know that you are a supernatural, divine creation of God?

# 5
# Overcoming Hurts

This is a very difficult chapter because it deals with very delicate circumstances in our lives. I personally have been through several traumatic experiences, some of which I can discuss in this book and others I cannot.

The reason I am telling you about some of my experiences is this: I want you to realize that because I have been through these tough, terrible things and have maintained a good self-image through them, I believe I can help you maintain a good self-image through *your* difficult times.

When we go through something traumatic or stressful in our lives, whether it's a rough childhood, or abuse, or a divorce, or drug addiction, or a bad sexual experience, or the loss of a job, or whatever it may be, it is a natural human tendency to pity ourselves, to feel sorry for ourselves, and therefore to develop a bad self-image. If you are at this point in your life, you now have a decision to make. Will you have a good self-image and go on to fulfill the dreams and goals you have for your life, or will you allow a bad self-image to take hold of you and keep you from ever obtaining what you have been reaching for?

You can't go around blaming the person who caused bad things to happen to you, even if that person is yourself. Forgiveness must take place. There must be a cleaning out so you can replace the "junk" that has been festering inside you with pure, good feelings about yourself, and forgiveness for the other person involved in whatever it was that hurt you.

I have met many adults, especially women, who were sexually abused as children. Many of them blame their 50 pounds of overweight, or their failed marriage, or whatever is wrong in their lives, on the fact that they were an abused child. Their self-image is always very low, because they don't realize that God can heal the hurt within them, and help them overcome that traumatic thing that happened in their lives.

Many times as I pray for people who are standing in prayer lines in services in which I am ministering, the Holy Spirit will tell me which of those people are being abused or have been abused in the past. And many times the persons themselves will weep and weep as they stand in that prayer line, because they are still carrying the hurt of that abuse, or the guilt of it, and can't forgive the one who caused it. Consequently that experience continues to eat them up inside. They are sick from it — sometimes emotionally, and sometimes even physically.

If you are going through sexual abuse (or some other kind of abuse) right now, I have something I want to say to you: you must realize that it is your life and that whoever is abusing you cannot do it to you any longer. You must understand that your abuser will love you even if you do put a stop to the abuse; if that person does not continue to love you, then he or she never loved you to begin with. Abuse is wrong, and you must make the decision to put a stop to it. You may have loved and trusted that person, but if he or she rejects you because you refuse to be abused any longer, God will replace that love you long for — just trust Him. He will *never fail you.*

If you have experienced any kind of abuse, whether sexual, verbal or emotional, you are not exempt from having your sense of self-worth restored to you.

I recommend first that you seek trusted Christian counsel — someone with whom you can verbalize this problem. Once it is verbalized, it becomes an exposed work of darkness, and the light of Jesus Christ expels darkness. This does not mean that you should broadcast your problem to everyone, but as it is shared with just one other reliable person, then it can be dealt with in prayer.

Second, recognize that you are or were a victim and not the guilty party. Satan will try to convince you that you deserve that kind of treatment. Recognize this as a lie. God sent His only begotten Son so that you can be free of false guilt.

The third thing you must do, and this is the most important of all, is that you must *forgive* the guilty party. This forgiveness can come as you ask Jesus to forgive *through* you, allowing His sufficiency to carry the load.

Your willingness to forgive will remove the roots of bitterness that can form deep inside you. If you try to just stick those memories back in your mind and forget them, instead of forgiving the person responsible for them, that unforgiveness will crop up like chopped off dandelions.

Many times we as humans react to hurts in our lives by just putting up a wall to protect us from them.

We try to shield ourselves from negative experiences so we never have to look back on them and be hurt by them any more. Or we try to just "scab over" our problems instead of bringing them out into the open so they can be healed. What we must do is pull off the scab and get rid of it. We don't need walls to protect our feelings.

By developing a good self-image, we can control what affects us on the inside. But we must also become very stable in our self-image, because the devil will try to fight us all the time. And the more we overcome those negative circumstances through a good self-image, the more we will be able to stand on our own two feet rather than having to seek approval from others.

There are negative situations in your life the devil uses to cause a bad self-image and which you need to dig up and get out. Once you get them out, they're really gone. But nobody can get them out but you. And sometimes it's a slow process. You've got to make the choice, and then you've got to do the digging. Nobody can dig them out of you, nobody but you can choose to get rid of them when they are found out. Then once they're gone, you can accept the healing God has for you.

You'll know when you've got total healing, because you'll be able to look back on your past life and view it as though it were another person's life you were looking at — like remembering a book you've read or a movie you've seen. This is what I call *healing of the memory.* The memories themselves are not erased, but the anxiety of those memories is wiped away.

Once this has taken place, with God at your side and His Word to guide you, your responses to life become true responses and not reactions to the hurts from your past. So you can face each day with confidence and a good self-image.

Be determined that you will settle for nothing less than total cleansing of these "roots." And when the devil comes back with accusations, remind him that you've already forgiven the person who caused you harm, and that everything has been taken care of. Let nothing destroy your good self-image in God.

No matter what happens to me in my life, I work very hard not to let it destroy my self-image. As you may know, I went through a divorce which ended my first marriage. The main reason I want to share this with you is because I hope that by doing so I will be able to show you how a good self-image can be maintained even in the sad situation of divorce through which so many people are going these days.

When I was growing up, I desperately wanted my parents' approval. The only problem was, it seemed to me that I could never get it. It wasn't that they didn't give me their approval — I just couldn't ever seem to feel that I had fully received it. Even though they never disapproved, they never outwardly approved either. No matter what I did, I felt I never made them happy.

Now remember, this is looking through the eyes of a child, and children are not always logical. My parents did all they knew to do for me, and were very proud of me and my achievements, but I just didn't realize that fact!

Before I won the Miss America title, I remember thinking, "I know, I'll win the Miss America Pageant; that'll make my parents happy." Then when I finally did win the pageant, they were still not overjoyed with me because my winning affected their lives also! It meant that we could no longer travel as a family group and sing together as we had done in the past. Now I would have to be on the road as Miss America, and that was a problem we *all* had to face. We all realized that things would *never* be the same again. But I could face that situation because I knew I was doing what God had called me to do.

Well, I finished the pageant years and came home, once again eager to win my parents' approval. As soon as I arrived at home, I began to see a man whom I had dated off and on for seven years. His family was very important to my family because they were probably the most famous natives of Choctaw County. The entire family had had a great influence on my life because they had introduced me to a deeper meaning of Jesus and to healing. I was especially close to the father of this family because of that introduction.

When death separated me from the father, I was devastated. It was then that his son came into my life and I transferred all of my affection for the father onto the son. So, every month or so for seven years, this young man would come to my family's home and spend the weekend with us, or I would go up to his family's place and spend the weekend with them. And that was the extent of our dating relationship over the seven years. We really never went out alone. Our dates were always a family-get-together type of situation.

In fact, the young man never really asked me to marry him. The way it happened was, one day we found a house we both liked and figured that if we were both going to live in it, we had to get married. There was no romance or courting.

He was 37 and I was 24, and it was the first marriage for both of us. I think he married me because it made everybody happy. It made my family happy and it made his family happy.

When we were married in 1981, I thought my family would finally approve of something I had done. And they did approve — they were thrilled. The only thing was that the marriage was a horrible mistake.

I think the very first time we had ever been alone together was on our honeymoon. We had never even talked to each other without a roomful of people around. It was a pitiful start for a marriage — just a sad situation. The whole foundation of the marriage was wrong in both of our minds. There were other difficulties, of course, but this was the root cause of our problem.

Once I realized what we had gotten ourselves into, I decided to just be positive and pray about the situation and confess over the marriage, and then everything would be fine. Well, I found out very quickly that positive thoughts and prayer and confession and all those things are wonderful, but they don't change people's wills. I could change my will, but I could not change my husband's will, nor could he change mine. No matter how much I prayed, no matter how much I believed, no matter how much I confessed, only he could decide for his own life, and only Cheryl could decide for Cheryl. There was nothing I could do to change him into what I thought he should be — and there was nothing he could do to change me into what he thought I ought to be.

Now here is where the situation really got hard. We had a very public life, and we were very good buddies. I was a big talker and a positive confessor. I could take any situation and turn it around and make it funny. So I decided to turn our "courtship" into a funny situation. I even did a lot of teaching on it.

The fact is, I thought what I was teaching was truth. I taught that if you pray and believe and confess something long enough, you will eventually have just what you say — just as I had confessed this man into marrying me.

And that's exactly what I had done. I had confessed that marriage into being. I had made it happen. That's why God warns us about getting snared by the words of our mouth. (Prov. 6:2.) That's why we've got to be careful what we ask for — because we could be asking for the wrong thing for our life. I had asked for the wrong thing, and I got the wrong thing — and it was a mess.

Well, we went from that point in our marriage to where we liked each other. We were friends. He was a tremendous musician, and I had great respect for his musical ability. We both played the piano well, so we played it together often. We went through that phase in our lives in which we did a lot of things that friends do — but we didn't do anything that a husband and wife do. We had more of a roommate relationship than a marriage. In fact, we just had no marriage at all.

Eventually I realized that we were living an incredible lie, and it seemed that nothing was going to change in our relationship. I realized that even though friends are friends forever (and you've got to be friends before you can be marriage partners), you can't *just* be friends if you want a real marriage. You have got to be husband and wife.

So I prayed and I believed and I went to two different pastoral counselors and also to a psychologist for about a year. One of the first pieces of advice I received was to do all that I knew to do — to stand firm, to pray, to believe, to do everything possible to save my marriage — then at the end of one year's time, if things were still no better, and if they didn't look as though they would be getting any better in the future, then I should walk away from the relationship, and walk away clean. After a year's time, after having done all I knew to do, and nothing had changed (if anything, things had actually become much worse), I took action. I left everything behind me — and I kept the news of my leaving out of the press.

The main thing I want to stress is that the basis of our marriage was all wrong in the first place. If I had allowed it to do so, our marriage would have totally destroyed my self-image! It would have also destroyed me!

One reason you may have a poor self-image in your marriage relationship is because you may be taking on yourself a lot of guilt that is not really yours. You may be taking blame for things that are not your fault.

Now that doesn't mean that you should go around casting stones at your mate and saying, "This is all your fault; it's your problem." All you have to do is just refuse to take the entire blame upon yourself. The Lord didn't tell us to go around pointing a finger at other people, but neither did He tell us to take their blame on ourselves. All He told us to do is to know the truth, to stand on the truth, and to be responsible for our own attitudes and actions.

I am responsible for me, Cheryl. And you are responsible for you. As Paul tells us in the book of First Thessalonians, each of us is responsible for our own happiness. We are responsible for praying without ceasing. We are responsible for being thankful in every situation. And when we get to the point where we can't do that any more, we are told not to quench the Holy Ghost because He will take over where our flesh is weak and He will make us happy — if we will allow Him to. He will pray and He will be thankful when we can't do it any more on our own.

What I want you to understand is that whether you're in the midst of a divorce or faced with a potential divorce situation, you should do absolutely everything possible to save your marriage. But if you've already gone through the divorce and it is behind you, then leave it there. The thing you must realize is, whether you were to blame or not, you have forgiveness — God forgives you.

You need to repent, to turn from your wicked way. When you do that, you can go to God and He will forgive you. Then you need to look from today forward, not from today backward. That is an absolute choice that you make. You look in the devil's face and you tell him, "Devil, you will not control me. You will not hold this divorce over my head. And you will not hold this experience in my memory! From this day forward I choose to live my life with a good self-image."

You've got to take responsibility, take charge, take control of your life and overcome the devil. Take your life out of the devil's hands, or he will run you around trying to destroy you.

Now there will be times when you will have to realize that you are not to blame for what is happening to you. The problem with your marriage may not necessarily be the fault of one individual or the other. Sometimes it may be like mine was, wrong from the beginning. My marriage was just a misconception from the very start. What we both conceived the marriage to be was just not there. I doubt if we even knew what marriage meant. I certainly didn't.

I had just finished my year as the reigning Miss America. I was emotionally torn up and tired out from traveling 364 out of the past 365 days. I had pretty much lost the identity of who Cheryl was, even though I had lifted up the Lord as I had planned. For one whole year I had been called Miss America — not even called by my own name. There were many times during that year when I looked people right in the eye and said, "My name is Cheryl Prewitt. My name is not Miss America. Miss America is my title; it is not my name. Call me by my name. My name is Cheryl." Of course, I was doing that out of frustration because I was gradually losing grip on my identity, of who I really was.

I had been advised not to marry anyone who had fallen in love with me *after* I had become Miss America. Instead I was told to be sure to marry someone who had loved me before I won that title. That way I was supposed to be assured that he loved me for who I really was. So I thought, "That's what I will do." And that's what I did!

He was right there waiting. I knew our marrying would please Mama and Daddy, and it would please his family also. Both of us married for the wrong reason — we were seeking the approval of others. I realize that fact now. But, of course, we all learn so much from hindsight, it's just amazing. If we can manage to get a grasp of the truth of a situation beforehand, rather than afterwards, it can sure make a difference in our lives.

Finally I reached a point in our marriage in which I lay on my kitchen floor and cried out, "God, I know that the whole world is telling me that if I go through a divorce, I can say goodbye to everything I am trying to do for You. Nobody will ever ask me to minister. Nobody will ever ask me to teach. Nobody will ever ask me to sing. I can kiss all that goodbye forever. But God, I am living an absolute lie — and I would rather live the truth and never be heard from again than to live a lie and have to tell it day in and day out just to save face. I just can't do that any longer."

Then I had to make a big decision. I had to ask myself: Am I, as an individual, more important than my ministry? And when I asked myself that question, it seemed like the most ridiculous question on the face of the earth. I realized that if I did not save myself, there was no hope of carrying on a ministry. I was slowly dying and was becoming something else . . . someone else . . . whom I didn't even know. I knew that if I didn't take the risk and save my own being, I wouldn't have a ministry left. Yes, maybe I could act and lie my way through life, but I couldn't have a ministry based on a lie. I was not being truthful.

It was then that I came to the point where I looked into God's face and said, "Lord, You didn't die for my ministry, You died for me. You didn't die for my traveling, my speaking, my singing; You died for me. You didn't die for Miss America; You died for Cheryl, the little girl from Mississippi, the little girl who had been hurt and who had felt as though she was at death's door time and time again.

"Lord, that's why You died for me . . . and that's why You sent me Jesus . . . and that's why I accepted Him . . . not so I could stand on a stage and be Miss America, but I accepted Jesus so Cheryl could live. But I'm not living, not like this. I'm dying. I'm slowly dying in this marriage."

So I got up, packed my suitcase, and walked out of that house. And I never looked back. I decided that Cheryl is worth something, and that's why I can tell you today, *you* are worth something. You are precious, you are vital, you are important to God. I don't care if you think other people feel that you are nothing. They do not matter, and they do not know. What matters is what you think, who you think you are, and who God knows you are.

That's what makes the difference. That's what makes a winner. That's what makes me an overcomer. That's what sets me apart. God says that He sets us apart for a certain work and a certain call. And the reason I'm set apart is because I had the guts to say,

"I don't care what anybody thinks of me. I don't care how many people turn up their nose at me. I don't care how many people cancel my concerts and seminars. I am vitally important to God as an individual. *Not* because of what I can do for Him, but just because I'm His kid, I'm important."

I know today that there are a lot of people in the same situation I was in, people who need to know that God cares about them and that He is vitally interested in who they are as individuals, not with what they can do for Him. God simply wants them — not their successes or failures. He wants their hearts to be submissive to Him, for only then can they truly have a good self-image — because then their self-image is based in God.

Now you may be wondering, "Cheryl, how can I ever maintain a good self-image when I'm hurting as you were?"

The first thing you must do is to let go of the hurt. Don't hold onto pain. As you release the hurt and pain, also release the person who caused them — whether it's your spouse or yourself — no matter who it is, release that person. Then let forgiveness penetrate and flood your heart. Only after you have done that can the healing power of God flood you from the crown of your head to the soles of your feet. He will heal you physically, spiritually, emotionally, mentally, and any other way you need healing.

This will help you to do the second thing you must do and that is to keep your prayer life very open to the Father. From the moment I realized that God died for Cheryl, and not for my ministry, and that He loved me as Cheryl and not just as Miss America, I kept the lines of communication open between my Father God and me. And I didn't let the devil come in and steal that communication from me in any way. (I will show you how to do this in your life in the chapter entitled "Delighting Yourself.")

The third thing you must do is get into obedience to God.

The Bible says that obedience is better than sacrifice. (1 Sam. 15:22.) Many times we try to make up in prayer what we lack in obedience, but it just doesn't work that way. God accepts our sacrifices (prayer, fasting, etc.) much more willingly if we're making a sincere effort to obey Him. If we continue in disobedience, many times we just hurt ourselves. Incorrect decisions can cause much hurt down the road — the only answer is obedience now.

You may be thinking, "But I've already been disobedient, and the consequences are coming back on me now!"

That is an unfortunate situation to be in, for sure. But, does that mean that you should remain in disobedience which only brings about more and more difficulty into your life? It's true that as you turn to obedience, God doesn't automatically wipe away all your problems by waving a magic wand, but He *will* point you in the right direction when you listen to His Word with an open heart and obey what He tells you to do. Then the hard part of getting over a divorce or restoring a failing marriage or going on with your life is made much easier.

When I lived in Nashville, a seventeen-year-old girl (let's call her Mary) was brought to me from an agency. She was pregnant, unmarried, and had come to this agency to give up her baby for adoption. When I first saw Mary, she was six months pregnant and had not gained any weight at all. She really was pitiful. She had no training, didn't know how to wear makeup or how to fix her hair (she just kept it pulled back in a ponytail). I could tell that her self-image was very low just by the way she looked down at the floor all the time and the way she just shrugged her shoulders when asked a question.

To make a long story short, with the help of my office staff, we led Mary to Jesus. Immediately she came alive and was like a different person. She let us show her how to fix her hair and how to apply makeup. She started eating properly. (Until then it seemed as though she was trying to starve her baby because she wouldn't eat anything.) I gave her a lot of clothes and showed her how to dress nicely.

But there were days when Mary would get down and would say, "I have accepted Jesus and He has worked out everything in my life, but I'm still carrying this baby." She would get very depressed over her situation, so I explained to her: "You accepted Jesus as your Savior and He has made you a new creature on the inside and has helped you to help yourself on the outside. But you are still pregnant because the consequences of your choice must be paid. They will be paid when you have that baby, and it is taken to live with another set of parents. You will have to put this mistake behind you. Even though God can heal the wound, that doesn't mean that the scar won't be there.

The baby does not disappear just because you became a Christian. The consequences of your choices have to be paid.

"Sometimes they are more severe, but other times they are paid in a lesser way. The fact remains that we pay the consequences of our choices. So it is important to know that the choice you make is going to affect the rest of your life. The key is that even though the consequences of our mistakes do not go away, our view of them and of our ability to deal with them greatly changes with Jesus in our heart."

I even let Mary talk to the girls, who were attending the charm school I was conducting at the time, about their choices and the consequences of them, and it completely changed her.

You too can choose to change right now, at this very moment. You can choose to get in line with God's Word — to bring your mind and thoughts into obedience to His will. This choice cannot change your past or present circumstances, but it will completely reconstruct your future!

We have no control over the past — we cannot change or correct it. We do have control over our future though, and for this moment on we can focus in on the . . . **mark for the prize of the high calling of God in Christ Jesus** (Phil. 3:14). This allows the present and future to be ruled by God's direction and His will as we walk in perfect obedience!

What I am saying is that we do not have to stay in disobedience. We make mistakes and we cause difficult circumstances by poor decisions in our lives. But we do not have to compound the problems by staying in disobedience and by continuing to make decisions out of God's will. Trying to correct one mistake by making another only means that we've made two mistakes. Obedience to God is the only answer.

God wants you to make this the greatest year of your life thus far. He wants you to stand up for His answer and say "No!" to the past and "Yes!" to His future in you.

You can rest assured that God will always take care of you during rough times. As I was going through this difficult time in my life, the Lord knew how I was hurting and how I felt alone, as though I was out there all by myself. He is always so good to give us just what we need, as we need it, to be there when we really need Him to show Himself. He didn't let me down.

One particular incident I recall, which is with me even today, took place in a wonderful church in Florida as I was ministering and singing a song written by Geron Davis called "Holy Ground." As I came to the part of the song which says "there were angels all around," I turned to my right and looked up toward the top of the church and saw a huge angel. He was so big and beautiful I just knew that everyone else could see him. He was pure white and quite muscular, with very dominant features. He was about ten feet tall — very vivid. He hovered over the congregation for about twenty minutes, and then he was gone. One thing in particular that I noticed about him was that he kept his arms crossed like Mr. Clean!

Later when I got on the bus with the ministry team that was traveling with me, I asked the Lord what the angel's name was and He told me it was Gabion. Then He told me that his name means "protector." And I remembered the protective stance the angel had taken when I saw him. It was as though the Lord was telling me, "No matter where you go, no matter what you do, no matter how many mistakes you make in this world, I am watching over you, child. I am protecting you. No matter how alone you may feel, there is Someone with you, and that Someone is Me . . . My presence . . . My angel." And the Father really assured me that He was with me at all times.

For three or four days I felt the presence of the angel, Gabion, just as you feel the presence of someone in the same room with you. He was constantly with me — everywhere I went, I felt him. Even now on some occasions I feel him stronger than on others, but now it's more of just a knowing. I know he's there. At times when I am feeling nervous, I talk to him and I say, "Now, Gabion, you know I'm feeling a little nervous. So this is your chance." And he always pulls me through.

Now here is the point: God is no respecter of persons. In other words, what He does for me, He will do for you. But there is absolutely no way I could have seen that angel if I had been wrapped up in self-pity and had a bad self-image because of what I was going through. You see, I never doubted that God loved me. And when you know that God loves you, you can truly have a good self-image.

Right now you may feel, as I did, that you are completely surrounded on all sides, that you are lost in the midst of a cloud of negative circumstances and that you will never find your way out again.

That's when you need to start believing that you can rise above those circumstances. (Is. 60:1 AMP.) Say, "Yes, I can rise above this situation." Stand up inside yourself . . . believe in yourself . . . see yourself in a good image. And, as you stand up, you are going to see God take His beautiful healing breath and blow away those clouds of circumstances that are surrounding you. They'll just disperse like smoke and go away. Now, the circumstances may not change, but your attitude toward them will.

This is your choice. This is your day. You can choose to rise above your circumstances. Right now, get rid of them. Get them out. Push them out. Hand them over to the Lord. Say: "Father, I want these circumstances out of me. I'm getting rid of them right now, in the name of Jesus. I'm just going to push them all out and let You heal me deep down inside."

That's what God wants you to do. He *wants* you to overcome, and He wants you to have an overcoming spirit within yourself so you *can* be an overcomer. And that's possible if you have Jesus in you. **Ye are of God, little children, and have overcome them: because greater is he that is in you, than he that is in the world** (1 John 4:4).

# 6

# Fighting for a Good Self-Image

Now once you have overcome the hurts of your past, the fight to maintain a good self-image doesn't stop there. It is a day-to-day process. But when you know that God is greater in you than the devil is in the world, you can't help but have a good self-image. You see, God can put our lives back together and guide us in a way we could never do on our own. I just sit back and marvel at what He has done and is doing in my life now.

Right after I moved out of our home, God began a healing process in my heart, in my emotions, and in my mind.

And in the midst of my healing, Richard and Lindsay Roberts asked me to appear on Richard's live daily television program. I agreed to do it, and when I did the show there was a good response from those who saw it. So several weeks later I was again invited to come to Tulsa and appear on the program.

This time, Richard and Lindsay asked me to have dinner with them after the show. As we sat down and began to talk, they asked me if I would consider staying on in Tulsa for a while and allow my healing to continue to take place there. (They knew about my painful divorce.) They explained that I would be able to take time to rest and just appear on the show when I wasn't traveling and ministering. I could enjoy a different nvironment from the one in which I had gone through so much hurt.

They wanted me to just be a part of their ministry family. So I agreed, and soon my healing was well on its way as Richard and Lindsay took care of me and prayed over me. God knew exactly what I needed, and He had opened the door for my inner healing to take place. But little did I realize just how much He was taking care of me.

In the course of my stay in Tulsa and my appearances on Richard's program, I met Harry Salem who was producer of the show. I saw him standing over on the side of the set every day, keeping the show going, and making sure that everything was running properly. I noticed him, but I still had so much hurt inside me because of my past that I had taken the position of not entering into a relationship with anybody. I wanted to leave everyone alone until I was completely healed of all my hurts.

Well, one day Harry took me to lunch with several of the people who worked for the Roberts' ministry. He loved to joke and laugh and we had a good time. It was then that I realized I *could* relax and have a good time *as* God was healing my hurt.

Not too long after that, Harry and I both knew that I was right for him and he was right for me. We had never even been out on a date, and yet we both knew we were to be together and that it was God's will. In my spirit I knew I was to be Harry's wife, and supportive of him, and also a part of the Roberts' ministry.

I heard from God; Harry heard from God; and we did what we knew to do. We didn't publicize our marriage; we didn't tell anyone about it — not even our families. In fact, my family didn't even know that we were dating. A couple of weeks later I just came home and told my entire family that I was married. I told them that it was God's will and that I had been obedient to that will. I said that I had not done this for myself or for anyone else, but simply because God had told me to do it.

I married Harry because I knew I deserved to be happy. I didn't care about approval from others. I didn't care what the world thought of me; I cared what God thought of me. I cared what *I* thought of me.

Now that may sound very calloused and hard, but I had to do this for myself — not to get approval, not to prove anything to anybody, but just for me, Cheryl. I deserved happiness. I deserved to be in the right place at the right time. I deserved to be living the truth and not a lie as I had been doing in my first marriage. I did not allow the bad decision I had made with my first marriage to ruin my self-image and cause me to make more wrong decisions. I had a good self-image and I knew I could make good decisions. I married the first time because of my need for approval. I married Harry because I knew it was what God wanted me to do, and it was what I wanted to do.

Now I'm not trying to paint a rosy picture of my new marriage. I'm trying to paint a truthful picture. I'm trying to show you how a good self-image can help make a marriage work. No, things are not always perfect. Our marriage is not always a bed of roses. I work at making this marriage successful, and so does Harry. We have our problems, as every married couple does, but the difference is, we face our problems with openness, honesty and truth. This makes a huge difference.

Before, I had become a very aggressive and self-sufficient woman. Harry is Lebanese and has very definite opinions about things. So when I decided to marry him, I thought, "How can I ever marry a Lebanese? He's a very dominant man of Middle-Eastern descent. He likes to take care of the woman, but for so long I have had to take care of myself."

That's when I realized that because of Harry's strength I could keep my own strengths without being "pushy." I could be exactly who God created me to be; I didn't have to try to be someone else. All I had to be was the woman God had called me to be.

I did not have to be domineering, but I didn't have to lose my dominant nature either. To be domineering means to be dominant over *someone*. To have a dominant nature means to be dominant in life — dominant over *circumstances* rather than over *people*.

Before I married Harry, I really never liked being dominant over people; however, I did like taking charge of my own life. But I never found that balance until I married Harry. Then I realized very quickly that I could still have a dominant nature and be dominant over my life, dominant over my circumstances, dominant over the devil, and take charge of every situation — *but* I never had to be dominant over anybody else. That revelation made me just relax and settle into my self-image and into the position that God had given me as

112

a Proverbs 31 woman — a woman who takes charge of the things that are in her *charge*. She has a very carefree nature in life, but she has control of the things she is supposed to have control over.

Harry showed me that this is possible, and is very natural and comfortable, because it's the way God set it out to be. God created man to be the spiritual head of the family. (Eph. 5:21-24.) He created woman to be submissive. That's why many times women are used more readily by God than men, because women have a natural instinct to be submissive — men do not. Men have to work at it.

We women, if we will allow ourselves, can fall completely into submission to the Father very quickly because He put that nature in us so we could be submissive to our mates. This is a good example of *how the way you look at something can change the total emphasis of it.*

For example, some women think the word *submission* is an ugly word, that it makes them a slave to their mate. This should *never* be true. Submission truly is a special bonus which God gave women — a natural, innate, God-given ability to hear His voice and to yield to it *naturally*. Men have to work at that. But if we women will just allow our natural submissive nature to come out, God can move through us faster and accomplish more than we can ever imagine!

So, very quickly I became submissive to Harry. I found out that when I do things for Harry (even when I don't feel like it), he is much more apt to do things for me, and this is just the principle of giving and receiving in action.

You see, submission does not mean inferiority or inequality. Submission without equality is simply slavery. God wants us to choose to be submissive. Then we work, move, and respond in love — as a servant, not as a slave! God does not intend for women to be slaves or else He would not have given them the wonderful capabilities He has. I found I could be strong *in* my husband, not in spite of him. Women must be spiritually strong too, so they can show the devil who's boss. Women have to do spiritual battle too! You have to fight for a good self-image on a continual basis. Just because I now had a good marriage, my spiritual battles didn't stop.

Soon after Harry and I married, I became pregnant. As soon as I found out, I remembered what the doctors had said to me years ago as a young girl after the accident — that I would never be able to have children. I knew God had healed me, and I was not going to let the devil steal my healing or this baby from me.

When I first got pregnant, I could have thought things like, "God, how will I ever carry this baby? How will I ever deliver him?" I could have thought all those fearful thoughts, but I didn't allow myself to. Instead I thought, "God, as many times as You've healed me, as many times as You have taken care of me, and as many times as You've proved to me that You can do a miracle, this is another one of those times."

You see, I did not allow the devil to lie to me and tell me I didn't deserve to have this baby and that I was a failure. I kept my good self-image and I decided that this time I wanted to give the devil two black eyes. I just wanted to lay him out good over this one! I was ready to do spiritual battle, because I wanted my baby to be anointed; I wanted him to be a big boy; and I wanted him to be mighty in the Lord. So every day I prayed over that baby inside me. Every day I called him "a child of the most high God," and "the child who hears the voice of the Lord." Every time I would move under the anointing, he would kick and move and get so excited!

Two months before I delivered Li'l Harry, I was ministering at Benny Hinn's church in Orlando, Florida, when Benny laid hands on me and said: "Yes, it's a boy and he's going to be anointed." Well, Li'l Harry just started kicking inside me!

You see, you *can* give the devil a black eye! But you had better be ready for battle because the devil will not quit. He will come against you till the bitter end. Just because you've beaten him once doesn't mean he will leave with his tail between his legs. He just backs up a little bit. Then he comes the next time running full force. That's why you've got to get your self-image established solidly in God.

I felt the devil's force when I went into labor to deliver Li'l Harry. I refused to let the doctors give me any medication because I had a point to prove to the devil. I had to get spiritually violent because the devil was coming against me to defeat me. I was in labor thirty-eight hours. My baby had become caught under my tailbone and couldn't get out. My doctor kept telling me that the baby was caught.

I said, "Just wait a minute . . . just wait a minute. We've got to get him out of there." The medical staff had to put a monitor on him because they were worried, but his heart was just fine. They finally broke my water and when they did they saw that it was green. From this they knew that there were complications which could cause Li'l Harry to be stillborn, but I could still hear that monitor going beep, beep, beep, beep, telling me that everything was okay.

Finally the moment came when Li'l Harry was born. He was perfect — absolutely perfect — eight pounds, three ounces. I tell you, I felt that I not only had given the devil a black eye, but I had knocked him out in round nine!

Harry and I named our son Harry Assad Salem III. *Harry* means "tiger" in Lebanese, and *Salem* means "peace." Li'l Harry is my Tiger of Peace. He will give the devil a run for his money because he is God's Tiger of Peace!

For all my children shall be taught of the Lord and great shall be their peace. (Is. 54:13.)

During this rough delivery of Li'l Harry, I could have slipped into fear and self-pity, but I chose to remember who I am in Jesus Christ and to just show the devil how great God's healing power really is. When He says He has healed me, I believe it!

Li'l Harry's birth was once again a miracle for me. He was a miracle for my husband also. When Harry was ten years old, his father died of leukemia, and he was never allowed the wonderful privilege of a father-son relationship. I think secretly he missed this so much! When Li'l Harry was born, it was truly as if God had restored to Harry the father-son relationship that he had lost as a little ten-year-old boy.

Li'l Harry was not only my miracle, but, also, his father's miracle — a restoration miracle!

Now I want to say a word to women who are going through a pregnancy or who will be in the future. I see so many women who have a poor self-image when they are pregnant, mainly because of the weight gain that takes place during this time. Let me tell you, this is one of the times in your life when it is most important to fight for a good self-image. That's the only way you are going to be able to take care of your body, spirit and mind properly.

The first thing you've got to remember is that your tongue is vitally important during this time. In other words, you can talk yourself into good, or you can talk yourself into bad.

Look at your body and think what a tremendous creation it is and how wonderful it is that God could make such a beautiful thing as a baby to grow inside you. When you think of it that way, it makes such a difference from thinking, "How ugly this body is, and how fat I'm getting."

A lot of what happens during this time has to do with the way you control yourself. If you let yourself gain forty, fifty or sixty pounds instead of twenty, you have lost your self-discipline. *Discipline is the key to a good self-image.* When you are not disciplined, you are out of control; but when you are disciplined, you are in control. Being disciplined will make you a much happier person.

As I carried Li'l Harry, I did not have any trouble. I only gained twenty-one pounds. Everything was wonderful. My pregnancy was beautiful, even though the devil tried to make me believe I'd never be able to have the baby.

Today I know that I am where I am supposed to be. That doesn't mean that circumstances are always easy. We are under the attack of the devil on a daily basis because of Harry's position as Executive Vice-President of Oral Roberts Ministries, and because of my position with the ministry and my own separate work — Cheryl Prewitt Ministry. But even though we are under constant attack, we are under constant victory also.

How do we keep a good self-image so we continally defeat the devil? We dwell in the secret place of the Most High, and we abide in the shadow of the Almighty. I pray Psalm 91 over my family every day, and I encourage you to do the same. This is how I pray:

> "Harry, Li'l Harry, and I dwell in the secret place of the Most High and abide under the shadow of the Almighty. We say of the Lord, He is our refuge and our fortress: our God, and in Him we will trust.

> "Surely He will deliver us from the snare of the fowler, and from the noisome pestilence. He shall cover us with His feathers, and under His wings shall we trust: His truth shall be our shield and buckler. We shall not be afraid for the terror by night; nor for the arrow that flies by day; nor for the pestilence that walks in darkness; nor for the destruction that wastes at noonday.

> "A thousand shall fall at our side, and ten thousand at our right hand; but it shall not

come near us. Only with our eyes shall we behold and see the reward of the wicked. Because we have made the Lord, which is our refuge, even the Most High, our habitation; there shall no evil befall us, neither shall any plague come near our dwelling.

"For He shall give His angels charge over us, to keep us in all His ways. They shall bear us up in their hands, lest we dash our foot against a stone. We shall tread upon the lion and adder; the young lion and the dragon shall we trample under feet.

"Because we have set our love upon Him, therefore will He deliver us: He will set us on high, because we have known His name. We shall call upon Him, and He will answer us: He will be with us in trouble; He will deliver us, and honor us. With long life will He satisfy us, and show us His salvation."

I quote Psalm 91 daily over myself and over Big Harry and over Li'l Harry. I do it every day because in verse 1 it says that we *dwell* in the secret place of the Most High. We don't just pass through there. We don't just visit there. We bring our toothbrush and our clothes and dwell there, which means we *live* there!

Also notice that we dwell in a *secret* place. Well, obviously God doesn't keep it a secret from us, because He has given it to us to live there. So it's the devil He is keeping it a secret from. He keeps our place of refuge a secret from the devil on our behalf. He cares about us that much — to literally give us a secret place in Him which the devil cannot find.

You can pray this psalm over yourself, over your mate, over your children — over your entire family.

Now you may be thinking, "Cheryl is happy now and everything is great, so it's easy for her to maintain a good self-image."

No, things are not always great. As I said earlier, our life is not a bed of roses. It's a constant struggle to keep God's gift; but we continually win, because we work at it.

In Philippians 4:11 Paul says, **Not that I speak in respect of want: for I have learned, in whatsoever state I am, therewith to be content.** And I am learning to be content every day. That is the proof to me that I am healed in my self-image from the past — the fact that I am learning on a daily basis to fight for my right to have a good self-image. It's my responsibility to take control of the situations that arise on a daily basis. I am learning that I can be in charge through the Holy Ghost in me, and that the devil can't lead me around by the nose if I don't let him.

How about you? Are you ready to fight for your good self-image and control your life? This is a decision that takes place on a daily basis. You make that choice again and again. It is a fight to the finish. It's not something you decide to do today, then never have to decide again. You have to continually decide; you have to continually fight for it; and you have to continually choose it. Yes, it gets easier, but it is still a fight. It never stops being a fight. It just depends on how much you are willing to give, how much it is worth to you. I want so much to see you get control of your life, to put the Lord in the driver's seat, to put the devil under your heel.

Just say right now, "In the name of Jesus, devil, you are under my heel. I put you there now, and in the authority of the name of Jesus, you will stay there. You will not raise your ugly head. Like it or not, the Word of God in me controls you, and I'm going to keep you down. You're going down for the last time, and you're not getting up any more. This is it for you, devil. You just lost the war. Get out of my life. Stay out of my mind. Stay out of my body. Stay out of my spirit. Stay out of my soul. I've got control over you because the Word of God lives big in me. And the authority in that Word is powerful because God spoke it into existence. And He gave it to me to use over you, so I do it now in the name of Jesus. Down, devil, down!"

Now take your heel and just rub it on his head. It'll do you good.

I'm so tired of watching the devil walk all over the Body of Christ. I'm tired of seeing him destroy the self-image of so many men and women when there is so much that God wants to do with their lives. Only through the Word of God can we come against what the devil is doing — not through our own strength. Try saying these words from scripture on a daily basis:

*"I am the body of Christ, and Satan has no power over me, for I overcome evil with good."* (1 Cor. 12:27; Rom. 12:21.)

*"I am of God and have overcome him (Satan), because greater is He that is in me, than he that is in the world."* (1 John 4:4.)

*"I will fear no evil, for You are with me, Lord; Your Word and Your Spirit they comfort me."* (Ps. 23:4.)

*"I am far from oppression, and fear does not come near me."* (Is. 54:14.)

Now as you set your spirit, mind, and body to fight for your good self-image every day so you can be what God wants you to be and to be successful as He has ordained, put on the armor of God and you will feel God's strength flood your spirit through His Holy Spirit and you will be dwelling in His secret place where the devil cannot harm you.

> **Put on the whole armour of God, that ye may be able to stand against the wiles of the devil.**
>
> **Stand therefore, having your loins girt about with truth, and having on the breastplate of righteousness;**
>
> **And your feet shod with the preparation of the gospel of peace;**
>
> **Above all, taking the shield of faith, wherewith ye shall be able to quench all the fiery darts of the wicked.**
>
> **And take the helmet of salvation, and the sword of the Spirit, which is the word of God.**
>
> **Ephesians 6:11,14-17**

Once you have done all that, *then* you will be able to withstand the devil and fight for your good self-image — . . . **and having done all, to stand** (Eph. 6:13).

# 7

# Becoming the Best You Can Be

It seems that recently we, as the Body of Christ, have grown a lot in our spirits, but we have neglected something very important — our bodies. The last few months the Lord has been showing me that He has a tremendous work for us to do as His children. And that job is going to require us to be complete, whole — in *body*, mind and spirit. Our spirit must be strong; our mind must be capable; and our body must be in good condition to be able to help us.

You see, your body is a vehicle for the Holy Spirit Who indwells you. It takes the Holy Spirit where God tells Him to go. Well, if you don't keep your vehicle fueled and serviced and properly maintained, then it won't go when He is "ready to roll"! There's nothing more aggravating, is there, than to get in your car all ready to go somewhere and find that it won't start? Well, you can imagine how frustrated the Holy Spirit gets with you when you don't keep His "car" in good running order!

Now if you should die, it will be wonderful to be present with the Lord, but you won't be able to do His work here on earth if your "car" gives out too soon. This is important to me because I don't want the devil to steal your physical body. It's wonderful if your spirit is in good shape. It's wonderful if your mind and your emotions and your soul are in good shape. But if your

123

physical body is dying, you need to do something about it.

I know this is not the most popular subject in the world. Believe me, when God told me to write about it, I said, "Lord, can't You tell someone else to do it? Don't tell me; I don't want to do it because it isn't a popular subject. No one wants to hear that he needs to get in shape." But let me tell you the exact words God told me to tell His people, especially His daughters!

"Take care of your body. How long do you plan on living under My grace with your physical body? When My grace is over, you will physically die."

That got my attention. It really got my attention. It makes you think of everything you put in your body, what you do to it, how properly you take care of it, how much rest you allow it to have, what things you allow it to eat.

I am sharing this with you because I want you to know that God cares about you completely. He cares about you wholly, and I think I am a perfect example of that fact. God cared for me enough to do what it took in my life to get me where He wanted me to be. You see, God had to do some special things in my physical body in order to get me ready to win the title of Miss America. After I was crippled from the car wreck, after my face had been through that windshield and received so many cuts it required over a hundred stitches to close them, God put me and my face back together again. And gave me a vision for you.

God cares about you. He cares about your physical body . . . He wants to heal you . . . He wants you well . . . He wants you whole . . . He wants you completed inside and out . . . *but* He wants you to do something about it too. He wants you to get up and discipline your life. He wants you to be responsible for your spirit, mind and body. He wants you to make the *right* choices. And if you make those right choices, listen to this promise from the Lord:

> **And may the God of peace Himself sanctify you through and through — that is, separate you from profane things, make you pure and wholly consecrated to God — and may your spirit and soul and *body* be *preserved* sound and complete . . .**
>
> **1 Thessalonians 5:23** AMP

I don't know what the word *preserved* means to you, but in Mississippi fruits or vegetables are *preserved* by putting them up in a jar or can so they will last a long time. That's what we call "preserves"! So that verse says to me that if I will make the right choices, God can do what His Word says He can do. He can preserve my spirit, He can preserve my soul, *and* He can preserve my *body* until He is finished with it. Do you want your body preserved until God is through with it? Well then, you have to do something.

Let me explain why this is important to me. It's important to me because when I went through that accident as an eleven-year-old girl, my body was nearly snatched away from me. I was crippled, and for all practical purposes, defeated in the eyes of others. But I saw myself as victorious, a winner, an overcomer, a becomer. So I care about your body, and I want you to be able to go where God tells you to go and do what

He tells you to do. I don't want you to stand before the Father and hear Him say to you, "If you had taken good care of yourself, I could have used you in so many ways and in so many places to carry My gospel, but because you didn't take care of yourself, I couldn't use you."

You see, I care about you and your physical body. You've got to take charge of your life. You've got to spiritually take charge of your life. You've got to emotionally and mentally take charge. And you've got to *physically* take charge of your life. Because if the spiritual is in great shape and the mental is in great shape and the emotional is in great shape, but the vessel that carries all those things around dies, "it ain't worth a flip." I know that's hard to swallow, but that's what God told me. I didn't argue with Him because it made good sense.

Now let me share some things that I believe will help you start doing what we've just been talking about — getting your body in shape so *you can become the best you can be.*

*Rest:*

I'm starting with rest because it's the most pleasurable of all the things we must do in order to keep our bodies in shape for what God has planned for us to do. And it is also the most overlooked thing God tells us to do. Many people do not realize how vitally important rest is for the mind and spirit and body. Your body needs time to revitalize, to rejuvenate, to replenish the everyday nourishments that are taken out of it as it keeps up with you all day long.

Sleep is essential if you are to be the best you can be. All people require different amounts of sleep. I personally need eight hours of sleep on a regular basis to be my very best. If I don't get that rest, it shows up in my voice, my skin, my hair — in every part of my body! That is why I want to stress the *regular basis* of that eight hours of sleep. That means that sometimes I can have seven hours of sleep and sometimes I can have nine. But if I go for a long period of time getting just two or three or four hours of sleep, eventually it will show up on me. And most likely my body will rebel and I will have to fight off a cold or some other illness that my body should not have had to fight if I had taken proper care of myself. And I'm sure this all true for your body as well. Our bodies are set up for an orderly routine.

You may be thinking, "Ha! That's a laugh. You should see my schedule and what I go through every day!"

Well, here is what I think of that: if I can come up with the time to be my best, you can do the best with what you have. I have a husband, Harry II, and a little son, Harry III. I travel 10 to 20 days a month which, of course, requires a lot of flying. (And airplanes can take a toll on your skin and your vocal cords because there is no natural moisture in the air.) I work on tapes, albums, aerobics videos, and books. I do television work with Richard Roberts on a daily basis. I have developed my own pageant swimsuit line called "Cheryl's Winners." I own this line, operate it, manufacture the swim suits, distribute them, wholesale them, and retail them. I conduct, *at least*, one all-day pageant seminar a month (often many more than that), and I run my own ministry with the help of one good secretary, Karen Jones. I answer my own mail (which is approximately fifty to one hundred letters a week). And I handle my own travel schedule, etc. In other words, I don't have a staff of people to keep me going. I do it all myself!

So if I can do all those things, you can do all you have to do and still be the best you can be *because you are important.*

*Just be aware of the ultimate best for you and continually strive for it.* You may never reach it, but if you are continually shooting for your very best sleep schedule, you are getting closer to your ultimate best every day.

*Eating Habits:*

Now here comes the painful part — or so many people think. You may have developed some eating habits that you know are not good for you; there may be some foods which you think you just can't live without. Well, before you skip over this section, let me encourage you to read what I have to say on this subject because I've got a feeling that once you start seeing what happens to your self-image when you begin turning yourself over to God physically, you'll be ready to do something about your eating habits. The rewards of what you will gain in your life will be so much greater than you've ever imagined — and all because you will have died to self and given this important area of your life completely over to Jesus. He'll do great things with it.

Now, along about here some of the men reading this book usually start thinking, "Well, I don't have to read this section because men don't have to worry about their weight like women do. We can afford to carry around a few extra pounds."

Let me tell you, that is one of the biggest lies the devil has ever told men — especially American men. God wants you to be around a long time with a healthy body so He can use you to do all the things He has planned for your life!

I discovered that being overweight or just physically unhealthy is as much a problem with men as it is with women! When I married Harry Salem, he was very slim. But after we had been married for a while, I became pregnant and during my pregnancy I gained twenty pounds — and Harry gained fifteen! He gained almost a pound for every one I gained. The only problem was that when I had the baby, my extra pounds went away, but he was still carrying his "baby" around!

I watched him as he would stand in front of the mirror and stick out his stomach and say, "I can't believe I let myself get in this shape." Then he would suck in his belly with all his might and turn this way and that. For six months I listened to him say, "Cheryl, I wish you would help get rid of this." Until finally one day he said, "Cheryl, I'm serious. Tell me what to do and I'll do it."

So I laid out a diet for him, but I told him I was not going to ask him what he ate every day or check up on him. If he was serious, he would have to be disciplined and do it on his own, because I knew that was the only way it would have a lasting effect on his self-image.

Well, he *was* serious and in two weeks he lost that fifteen pounds and has kept them off ever since. You might say, "That's impossible!" No, it's not. That's discipline.

Now let's discuss what you actually need to do to keep your body healthy with good eating habits. Personally, I'm not a breakfast eater, but I do highly recommend that if you like breakfast, eat it. I just can't stand much on my stomach early in the morning, but if you can handle it, breakfast should be your main meal. That is the time to get your nutrition — but don't overeat. The American body does not need to be overloaded. Just eat healthy and what is *good* for you.

For lunch eat plenty of fruit and vegetables, but very little meat, especially red meat. Do you know that red meat contains over one hundred calories an ounce? Now that's a lot of calories for the amount of meat, especially since it stays in your digestive system such a long time. If you need protein, instead of eating red meat, it's really better to eat chicken or fish, cheese, eggs, or peanut butter. (But go easy on the peanut butter because it is very high in calories).

All I have to say about sweets is . . . try to stay away from them, period!

Keep your breads to a minimum. You do need some grains, but the problem with most people and their "bread eating" is that they don't eat the right kind of bread. They don't eat wheat or other *whole grain* breads. Instead, they eat white and very thick bread. Unfortunately, white bread contains four basic ingredients which are all very bad for you: white flour, white sugar, white salt, and white lard.

None of these things is good for your body, though I will agree that when they are mixed together, they do have a great taste. But I must tell you that they are not good for you. In fact, they are not good for any part of your body "healthwise." And, believe it or not, you don't need those things to keep you alive! If you do not like the way you look, cutting those four things out of your diet will make you look better because they take away the healthy, fresh look from your body, skin and hair!

Now if you are trying to lose weight, let me give you a brief menu and some tips to help you. First of all, you don't need over 1000 to 1200 calories a day. In my case, I try my best to eat no more than 500 to 800 calories daily. Some people may say, "That's not healthy." Well, it works for me, and I'm healthy.

Also, if you're trying to lose weight, you need to eat *early* in the day so your body will have time to digest your food while your metabolism is still going strong. Once you get to bed, your metabolism slows down, and if you've eaten late, the food will turn to fat. It's best not to eat after 5:00 p.m., but for sure don't eat after 7:00 p.m. You'll find that if you can make yourself go to bed early and go to sleep, you'll miss much of that hunger time when most people start "pigging-out" and snacking late at night.

Now here is a brief menu I believe you will find helpful as a guideline.

*Breakfast Menu:*

If you can eat some wheat toast, half a grapefruit, maybe some kind of grain cereal or a boiled or scrambled egg (cooked with very little oil), you've got a fabulous breakfast. On that wheat toast you need to leave off butter, jelly, or peanut butter. Breakfast should be your biggest meal. *Eat what you need, not what you want.* I know that sounds impossible, but once you have a good self-image founded on God's Word, you'll find that you can do it. And you'll find that you will like yourself much better.

*Lunch Menu:*

Lunch should be your biggest meal, if you eat as I do — no breakfast. Ideally, breakfast should be the biggest meal, lunch should be next largest, then supper or dinner (depending on what area of the country you come from) should be the smallest meal of the day. Since I don't eat breakfast, I try to have a nice meal at lunch. If I'm going to eat protein that day, that's the meal at which I try to eat it. I have a nice salad and I try to eat fruit. In fact, it is nice if you can eat fruit at every meal.

*Dinner Menu:*

Then at dinner, especially when you are trying to lose weight, it's nice if you stick with fruit. (I'll show you later how exercising before dinner will break your appetite). I like to eat an apple for my dinner. That's usually all I want after I have exercised. Even if I'm going out to eat, I keep it to a minimum — a salad and a fruit. Eat very, very light at your evening meal and heavier at your earlier meals. If you feel that you must eat more for dinner, some other alternatives are a baked potato with one ounce of cheese (not butter or sour cream), a nice tuna or chicken salad, or a piece of chicken or fish broiled or baked with very little oil.

*Junk Food:*

Now, I want to talk to you about a killer! Junk food is just that — an unusable, non-nutritional, justifiable (those who love it try to justify it!) killer! It's bad for your body in any amount, and most people overindulge in it terribly. *Don't be one of those people.* Love your body as God does. Eat right. Take a multiple vitamin, drink juices, drink water, and stay away from diet drinks if at all possible. In fact, all carbonated drinks are not very good for you, especially if they have salt in them. Eight eight-ounce glasses of water are still a wonderful idea if you can make yourself drink them, especially if you are trying to lose weight.

When I was getting ready for the Miss America Pageant, each day I ate an apple, a piece of meat, a piece of cheese, and a salad with nothing on it. Salad dressing is the worst thing you can eat when you're trying to lose weight. So many people go on a diet and don't lose weight. Then they'll say, "All I'm eating is soup and salad, soup and salad, soup and salad, yet I'm getting bigger all the time." That's because soup and salad are the worst things you can eat on a diet because most people just pile on the salad dressing and add extra salt to the soup. Even if you don't salt your soup, there's usually already enough in it to hurt you. Soup is full of salt. So when you eat it, you can't get rid of the water in your body. Don't eat soup when you're trying to diet and don't eat salad dressing or mayonnaise. Don't eat those things, because they're terrible for you.

It's called discipline. Your body needs to learn who's boss. For two years I kept a sign on my refrigerator which read: *"I don't desire to eat so much that I become overweight. I present my body to God. My body is the temple of the Holy Ghost which dwelleth in me. I am not my own, I am bought with a price. Therefore, in the name of Jesus, I refuse to overeat. Body, settle down, in the name of Jesus, and conform to the Word of God. I mortify the desires of this body and command it to get in line with the Word of God."* (Rom. 12:1; 1 Cor. 6:19.)

Every day I present my body to God as a living sacrifice. My body and your body house the Holy Ghost, therefore we had better take care of them. Jesus lives in us. Remind yourself of this truth with a note. Realize that it is not insulting to your intelligence to put little signs up to remind you of important things to remember.

I am on the Richard Roberts' show now, and the theme of the program is "Turn It Around." And Richard has put that on a little plaque. I thought that would be great to put on the refrigerator — when you start to open the door, you see "Turn It Around." Then you turn around and walk off and leave that junk food alone. You don't need it. Stay away from it.

*Exercise:*

The problem with people losing weight is that they will lose 10 pounds and gain 10 pounds, lose 10 and gain 10. They end up losing and gaining 100 pounds a year. The reason for that is they never change their *setpoint.*

134

Your setpoint is basically what your body wants to weigh. It has weighed that for a long time, so it's used to weighing that amount. All your body functions are used to that certain weight, so when you drop 10 pounds, and you drop it pretty fast, if you don't exercise your body, when you start eating normally again you will gradually gain right back up to your setpoint.

The only way you can change your setpoint is to exercise. Truthfully there is probably no way to lose weight and keep it off successfully without exercise. The best thing I've learned in the last few years to do for my exercise is aerobics.

Perhaps you prefer something like walking. It was reported in a health magazine that if you walk thirty minutes a day, just as fast as you can, in a year's time your body will drop 20 pounds without your ever changing your eating habits.

But you know, the problem with that for most people is when they start walking that thirty minutes each day they think they can eat an extra amount each day too. They think that just because they're exercising regularly, they can eat more. Well, you can eat more, but you'll probably stay about the same weight!

So to change your weight or to stay healthy, you must exercise. And I don't mean to exercise your heart out today and then not exercise at all for two weeks. You must exercise the same amount every day on a diligent, regular routine.

The first thing you need to do is to set a realistic goal for yourself. A lot of people, especially American women, have gotten a little crazy with the idea of being thin. I mean, there are some women you have to paint to see them! It's ridiculous.

I just put on 10 pounds on purpose because I had gotten way too thin. I realized all of a sudden that it made me look old, and I didn't like that. Being too thin can make you look older than you are, because the first place that you're going to get thin is not in your hips, it's in your face and neck. So don't drop your weight to the point you look anoretic. You'll look like a chicken head sticking up through your clothes! It's terrible. I decided to gain 10 pounds so I would feel much better.

Now I didn't stop my exercising and I didn't gain weight by eating junk food. I put the weight on by eating normal meals, watching what I was eating. And I put it on gradually because gaining or losing anything in a hurry is bad for your heart. It puts a strain on your body. So whether you are gaining or losing, do it gradually and in moderation. The Bible says to let your moderation be known to everyone. (Phil. 4:5.)

Here are some little keys to exercising. I like to do aerobics for exercise because I can do them in thirty minutes. I also like to ride a stationary bicycle. So if for some reason I can't do the aerobics, I ride the bicycle. Most people, if they really want to, can find thirty minutes every day to exercise. I look at it this way: if you can find an hour and a half to eat, surely you can find thirty minutes to exercise. Right? Thirty minutes is really not that hard to find.

You may decide to exercise in the morning or at night before you go to sleep. Some people can't exercise at night because they can't sleep afterwards. I can go to sleep easily after I have had a nice aerobics workout and a long hot bath. I sleep like a baby. I hate getting up first thing in the morning and doing aerobics. I just can't "get into it" that early. My favorite time for doing aerobics is about 5:00 or 6:00 p.m. I do my exercises instead of eating supper because, you see, when you exercise it takes away your hunger.

Contrary to popular belief, when you do thirty minutes of heavy exercise, you do not get hungry from it. Now you may get hungry a few hours later, but just tell yourself, "I don't eat after 7:00 p.m. Sorry, body." Then drink a cup of hot water. It will curb your appetite, clean out your system, and make you feel good.

Now another reason the prime time to do your exercise is between 5:00 and 6:00 at night is because that is when most people get the "munchies" or the "hungries." They're just starved about that time of day. But if you will put your exercise in place of eating, you'll find that you'll lose weight very quickly, because the evening meal is the one that puts weight on you. Don't worry, you're not going to hurt yourself at all by doing this, if you eat breakfast and lunch. Your body will do fine.

Now let's talk about what you should wear when you exercise. When I do my aerobics, I put on a heavy pair of *plastic* pants and a pair of dancer-size pants on top of those. (I don't wear the plastic pants for long periods of time because they're not good for your skin since after a while they close up your pores.) Then in the wintertime I put on a heavy pair of sweats on top of all that. So I have on three pairs of pants and heavy socks. You see, I'm not doing aerobics to look cute in my little aerobics outfit. I'm doing aerobics because I want to get my heart rate up so my body will sweat and clean out my system. My metabolism goes up real high and burns calories. If you don't get hot and sweat when you exercise, your metabolism is not going to go up. When you get real hot, you're not "dewing" and you're not "perspiring" — when you have on three pairs of pants, you're *sweating*!

And when you put on three pairs of pants, you don't want anybody to see you because they will definitely tell you that you need to go on a diet! It's not pretty. It's not glamorous. It's not "nice." And it's not even fun — at first. *But you can make it fun when you learn that you're controlling your body.*

I don't want my mind in control, I don't want my body in control, I want my spirit in control. When I first started getting into shape, I had to fast a little — not to lose weight, but to teach my body who was boss. Now you may not need to do that. You may have tremendous self-control. I didn't. So I fasted for a little while just to teach my body that I will tell it what to do. It will not tell me. I will tell it. Again, if you decide you need to fast to gain control over your body, do it moderately. Don't be unwise and make yourself sick. You'll defeat your purpose before you really get started.

Remember, exercise is very important if you ever want to change your setpoint. You can lose all the weight in the world, but you'll probably put it right back on if you don't exercise.

Now sometimes people don't even lose weight when they're exercising, but rather their body weight shifts around. You will need to take this into account when you're deciding what to wear during exercising. The reason I wear three pairs of pants instead of three shirts is because from my waist down I always need to lose weight. Most women do. Most are built like a pyramid rather than like an ice cream cone! But you have to find out what works for you.

Usually there are several goals that people have in mind for their body when they're exercising. You may be working on spot reduction. For example, to get ready for the Miss America Pageant, I had to work on the top of my legs. So I got a stationary bike, raised the seat as high as I could get it, placed a towel on the floor (because of the sweat), put on some sauna pants, released the tension on the bike, and then peddled for at least an hour every day without stopping. Now if you decide to do this, to really lose inches in a short period of time, you can peddle two to three hours a day. This will do the trick for you.

But I must tell you about two aerobics videos I have recorded that I believe can do for your body what you need done! The first video is called "Take Charge of Your Life." It's very active and is usually for younger people; however, Daisy Osborn, a 62-year-old woman who is a famous evangelist and the wife of T.L. Osborn, does this aerobics video every day! So it really depends on how active you currently are. The second aerobics video, "Getting Ready," is a little slower and only lasts 28 minutes. On both of these videos I encourage you with scriptures and play spiritual music during the exercises.

These videos are the best ideas God has ever dropped into my heart. People all over Amercia are getting turned on to Holy Ghost exercise. Let your spirit rise up and take charge of your body. If you would like to order one of these videos for $25, there is information at the end of this book that will tell you how you can do that. And when you get the video, don't just watch it — *do* it!

Now when you do aerobic exercise, you may want to do it with somebody. Exercising with somebody is great, but you must make sure that the other person doesn't become your motivator. I personally don't care whether anybody wants to exercise with me or not. I am going to do it anyway because I know what it's doing for my body.

Remember, exercise is good for your cardiovascular system. It gets your heart rate up and challenges your body. It also makes you sweat out impurities and gives you more energy than ever before.

It is also necessary for toning up your body — which everyone needs — whether or not they need to lose weight. Aerobics and spot reducing can help you tighten and tone your body faster than anything else you can do. And you can do these at home with my aerobics videos!

*Posture:*

Standing:

Now I want to talk to you about your posture. Did you ever see anyone with a good self-image go around with a slumped posture? No way, because people with a good self-image hold their head high and stand straight. They know where they're going.

In order for you to look your very best, your posture must be good. It is of the utmost importance. You need to stand very tall, as if someone were pulling you up with a string running right up through your tailbone, on up through the back of your spine, up through your neck, and right out the top of your head. If you will do that, you will get every inch of your height and even more.

I'm only 5′5″ tall, but I've been told repeatedly that I look taller than that. People always guess my height as 5′7″ or 5′8″. I appear taller because I stand every inch of my height.

You can change the way you look just by the way you stand. Standing correctly can make a lot of difference in the way you appear to others and in the way you perceive yourself. Without realizing it, many people stand in a slightly slumped position. So I encourage you to stand in front of a mirror as I give you some tips on what to do to improve your posture.

The first thing you need to do is to remember to pull your shoulders back — not up, but back. Now when you do that, you're probably going to think, "Oh, my back is killing me." That's because you've had such terrible posture for so long. But even though it's uncomfortable at first, get in the habit of keeping your shoulders back. Remember that you must break old bad habits and establish new good ones. Rebuke the pain in the name of Jesus and stand up straight.

Now while you are in that position feel where your rib cage is. Is it down or is it up? If it's down, pick it up. That will straighten up your body and give you the appearance of another two full inches in height. Keep your rib cage up and your shoulders back. You will look younger and healthier! You'll also find that you will breathe better and have more energy because you'll be getting more oxygen.

Now when you pick your rib cage up, you'll have a tendency to stick your hips out. To avoid that, you just roll them under. Just move your hip bone under your spine. This posture can take about three inches off the appearance of your hips. You'll also find that when you roll your hips under your body, your stomach seems flatter.

A good way to practice proper posture is to place your back against a wall and roll your hips, shoulders, and back all the way over as you bend down and touch your toes. Then place your hips right back up against the wall. Now roll your spine up one vertebra at a time until every part of your back is flat against the wall. There should not be any space between your back and the wall, from top to bottom. When you get to the point you can do that, then step away from the wall, holding your body in that position.

Besides improving your appearance, this way of standing is good for your back. I believe people would need less healing for their backs if they would learn to stand up correctly.

Some people have everything just right in their posture, but they stick their head out. As you stand erect, pull your head back in line with the rest of your body. Line up everything from the top of your head to the bottom of your feet — one good straight line. This way you will always have an extremely "straight-up-and-down" look.

Walking:

I hate to say this, but it seems that most people need to learn how to walk properly! I know they learned when they were about a year old, but they probably walked better then than they do now; often people get into bad habits and don't realize it.

One of the bad walking habits I see in many people is their tendency to gallop like a horse. They just kind of push off with their feet, taking giant strides. They step out too far and then have to pull their body along to keep up.

Then I see some people who allow their body to carry their legs. What I mean by this is, they lean over when they walk, pushing their body out ahead of their legs.

But there are those who do worse — they let their legs carry their body! When they walk, they look as if they are always late!

If you will practice correct posture when walking, keeping your body and legs in straight alinement, all of these problems should correct themselves. Just hold yourself erect at all times and you will automatically walk properly.

So many women walk with their feet side by side. That is the way men walk; it is not flattering to a woman. It makes her look "square."

Walk as if your heels are on a straight line, turning your toes slightly to the outside. Put one foot directly in front of the other. Your left heel should touch down, then your right heel should be brought forward in front of your left foot, touching down in line with where your left heel was previously set. As you walk, turning your toes slightly to the outside (a couple of inches) gives you a beautiful long line.

You may think this sounds like ballet. Well, it is just like ballet: heels in, toes out.

Don't take long steps. If you're in a hurry, instead of taking bigger steps, just walk faster. Always walk briskly. Don't stroll along. You'll miss everything. Get in a hurry. It will help your metabolism and therefore help you lose weight. I do everything in a hurry. Now that doesn't mean that I run through life, but I don't drag along either. Life is too short. We have got a lot to do. Let's go! Get with the program. Jesus is coming back and we've got to hurry and do what He has called us to do.

Now let's talk about going down steps. Most people walk down steps with their head down the whole time. Those steps aren't going to jump out from under you, and they're not going to change. Usually the rest of the steps are just like the first one. So take a good look at them before you start down, and *then* you can descend without having to look down at your feet constantly. If you need to glance down occasionally, do so quickly, but don't look down the whole time. If you do, it will look as though you are not in control.

So when going down steps, get a good look at them before you start down, then just descend them with grace and confidence!

If you are going up steps, criss-cross your legs. In other words, don't walk with your legs spread apart. Some people do this because they think it gives them a good foundation. Criss-cross your legs. It looks so much prettier. By criss-cross I mean, lead with one hip, followed by the other, walking sideways. It makes you appear thinner and gives you a nicer look. Plus, you will have much better control while going up steps.

Remember, when you're walking, stand very tall and keep your head back, not bent over. Don't lean forward, and don't lean backward. Stand erect, with your rib cage up, your hips rolled under, your stomach tight, your shoulders back, and your head up. As you walk, place your heels as if you are walking on a straight line, and turn your toes out ever so slightly, just a couple of inches. This will help you walk correctly.

Look at yourself in the mirror as you try walking this way. You'll be surprised at the difference it makes in your appearance. If you will practice walking correctly, eventually it will become natural to you.

Sitting:

When you start to sit down, do not stick your hips out as though you are searching for the chair with them! Bend your knees just in front of the chair and, keeping your back straight, lower your body to the seat.

When you get up, do the same thing in reverse. Don't push off with your hands or scoop up like a bird ducking for a fish in the water. Just stand straight up. Your body is not the Titantic. You don't need to use all your weight to pull it up. Make your legs do all the work.

In fact, a wonderful way to practice sitting and standing is without a chair. Bend your knees as if sitting, then straighten your legs as if you were rising from your seat. Bend your knees to sit, then straighten your legs to stand.

Practice this procedure, going directly up and down, and you'll soon get into the habit of sitting and standing properly. Remember: the chair will not move. If you've looked, and it's there, it will still be there when you lower yourself onto it. Feel it with the back of your legs, then sit down gracefully and confidently. Rise up the same way. It's not a lot of work. Just keep your back and head straight.

While sitting, if you want to achieve the ultimately beautiful look, cross your legs at your ankles and fold your hands in your lap, especially if you are at an important meeting or if you particularly want to look your best. (Of course, I think you should always try to look and act your best, regardless of the circumstances or situation.)

When seated in an important meeting or interview, don't get too comfortable or slouch in your chair. But you don't need to be stiff. Sit up straight, be respectful, but just be yourself.

When the meeting or interview is over and you start to stand up, first uncross your ankles. You would be surprised at how many people try to stand up with their ankles crossed. You can hurt yourself doing that. Uncross your ankles, then stand straight up.

Now about body language: posture is one of the most important communicators of body language. If you have good posture, you give people the impression that you feel good about yourself . . . that you're happy with yourself . . . that you're pleased with yourself . . . that you feel that you are in control. This makes people feel comfortable with you. Nobody likes to be around someone who is down or sad or depressed or shy. Why? Because it makes them feel uncomfortable. That's not to say that they don't like people who have a poor self-image. They may love them. But a poor self-image makes others uncomfortable and most people try to avoid feeling that way. A good positive stance or posture is positive body language.

You can use your face to improve your appearance and your appeal to others tremendously. A smile is the most positive thing in the world. Sometimes you can just smile with your eyes. You can express what is on the inside of you by the look in your eyes, because your eyes are truly the widow to your soul. So smile with your eyes.

Use your eyes to your advantage. Always look people in the eye when you're talking to them. (I say "eye" instead of "eyes" because it's only possible to look at one eye at a time.) Try it. People feel comfortable with you when you talk directly to them.

I have a friend who is a wonderful lady. But the whole time she talks to me she looks up. She can be standing right in front of me, or across the room from me, but she won't look me in the eye. She'll always look up. Sometimes I want to say to her, "Hey, I'm down here. Talk to me right here. I'm not going to hurt you."

I want to be talked *to*, not *at*. Look at the person to whom you're speaking. Look him right in the eye. It makes the other person feel comfortable and lets him know that you're confident about yourself.

Think about eye contact when you're sharing Jesus with somebody. If you can't look someone in the eye when you talk to him, he will wonder what you are ashamed of or what you are hiding. Aren't you proud of Jesus? Aren't you glad to know Him? If you've got a sad, ugly face because you're down about something, then don't try to share Jesus with others that day. He doesn't need that kind of witness. He's a happy Jesus. So smile and be happy. Share your inner person with people.

*Clothes and Makeup:*

Clothes are important to your self-image because they can make a big difference in how you look and how you perceive yourself. Here are just a few *nevers* about clothes:

1. NEVER accentuate the negative about yourself or anyone else. Always accentuate the positive.

2. NEVER dress "fadish" — especially if the fad is not flattering on you. There is nothing wrong with wearing fadish clothes, but never wear something just because it is the "latest style" or the "in thing." Choose clothing which emphasizes *your* best qualities, not someone else's.

3. NEVER wear clothing that is too tight-fitting. When your clothes are too tight, they usually accentuate the negative — your worst features — not the positive — your best. (Just a little secret I discovered: when I wear a slightly larger size, I look smaller!)

4. NEVER wear horizontal stripes, unless you want to look like a barrel! Avoid stripes that go around rather than up and down. Vertical stripes make you look taller and thinner.

5. NEVER wear shoes that are of a lighter color than your clothing, unless you want your feet to look huge! Wear lighter-colored shoes *only* if you want to accent your feet. Match the color of your outfit with your shoes or go with a darker color — never lighter.

6. NEVER wear low-heeled shoes if you are short and want to seem taller. Choose shoes with a higher heel. Even a small heel, when worn with casual clothes, will make you look taller and cause you to stand up straighter.

7. NEVER wear slacks that are too tight. The tighter your slacks, the bigger you look in them.

Since it is so important, I want to emphasize again that you should never wear your clothes too tight. I have found that clothing worn just a little loosely will give the illusion that you are thinner. And, of course, everyone wants to look thinner. I know very few people in this world who want to look heavier. The majority of people would rather look thinner. (Obviously, the best solution would be to actually lose a little weight, but if you don't, or until you do, try using this illusion.)

Wearing clothes that compliment your coloring always makes you look better. I have had a color analysis done and have been classified as "winter." I would recommend treating yourself by having someone do a color analysis of you. (Don't pay a lot for it, because many times you can just be paying for someone else's opinion; but nonetheless, there are times when it can be helpful.) Go ahead and pamper yourself a little and have it done.

But remember: your best clue for which clothes look best on you is how you feel and how people respond to you when you wear them.

For example, if every time you wear a certain color, you receive a lot of compliments on your appearance, then that may be a good choice for you. However, if when you wear that color, you are asked if you are not feeling well, you can probably take that as a clue that you should avoid that color or shade.

If you have a long neck, as I do, you should never wear clothes with a long, thin neckline. By that I mean a neckline that leaves your neck and chest open — for instance, a "V" neckline. I don't look good in that design of clothing so I don't wear it. Likewise a short haircut is not good for you if you have a long neck; unless, of course, you want to emphasize your neck. Some people do like to do that to a degree.

Concerning shoulder pads: I have very thin, narrow shoulders, but fortunately shoulder pads are in style right now, so I have a wonderful opportunity to help balance out the top and bottom of my body. The opposite will be true for you if you have wide shoulders. In that case, do your best to avoid clothes with padded shoulders, or else you will end up looking like a football player!

*Remember to spotlight the positive, not the negative.*

If a small waist is your greatest asset, show it off! A belt is a nice accessory for the small waist. If large hips are a problem for you, wear full shirts that hang prettily and are flattering to your figure. Also, a straight, long skirt with a long top over it can help camouflage large hips. Avoid tight knits. They cling to the worst areas of the body. Show off your "positives" and hide your "negatives."

Many ladies ask me about short hair. They want to wear their hair short, but wonder how they can still look feminine. First of all, a person with short hair should keep it from lying flat against the head. A proper cut and regular shampooing and conditioning are essential in order to give short hair that body and bounce it needs to look pert and lively. Nice-sized earrings (not gawky-looking ones) with a good color and sparkle to them will add a lot to short hair. Also using a bit of extra color in your makeup (being careful not to overdo it) will help make a shorter hairstyle more feminine.

Because of the current styles, full-figured ladies are fortunate right now, especially those who are carrying a little too much weight or have a "boxy" build. Long tops and coats, and sweater tops with matching skirts, are all really popular at the time of this writing. And even if they are not "in" at the moment, wearing them will make you look smaller and taller. Also, wearing the same color nylons and shoes can make you look taller because a single shade draws the eye up and down in one long smooth vertical line.

Now here are a few *nevers* about makeup:

1. NEVER wear a base makeup (foundation) outside of your general color sheme. It's popular now to choose makeup according to your "color" or "season" — winter, summer, spring or autumn. You may fit nicely into one of these categories, or you may not. But in either case, try to keep within the basic color scheme which goes with your complexion. From time to time you may want to change your eye makeup, your blush, or even the color of your

clothing, but your basic foundation needs to always be in your color scheme. (It's called foundation for a reason!)

2. NEVER leave a makeup line on your chin, jaw or neck. (A makeup line is evident when you can see where your makeup begins and ends.) To avoid leaving an unsightly line, smooth out the edge with a sponge.

3. NEVER go out of the house without wearing your base makeup. This is not so you'll look better, but for the sake of your skin. Your face needs protection against dirt and dryness caused by a lack of moisture in the air.

4. NEVER sleep with your makeup on; it's damaging to your face and skin. You may say, "But I just do it now and then; I don't always have time to wash it all off." Love your face and your skin. Do them — and yourself — a favor. No matter how tired you are, never go to bed without carefully removing your makeup.

5. NEVER wear too much eye makeup. You might look like a streetwalker! Wearing too much eye makeup draws attention to your makeup, not your eyes. It overdoes instead of doing just enough.

The next most important thing I can say to you about your face is — take care of it. Don't abuse it with makeup. Depending on your coloring and your age, the choice of your base makeup (foundation) may be the most important decision you make because it affects how your entire face looks.

Here are some practical tips about makeup: Use a sponge when applying makeup, especially if you have oily skin, because your fingers have oil on them. Make sure you move the sponge along the chin line and even down the neck if necessary to keep from leaving a makeup line.

Never overdo your makeup. A little goes a long way. Just enough is best. During the daytime, wear less makeup. At night, you may wear a little more.

The way you apply your base and blush affects your entire facial features. For instance, if you have high cheek bones and a thin nose, do very bare shadowing. Use darker blush. Shade darker base on the bridge of your nose on both sides, and just under your cheek bones (the hollow of your cheek).

Concerning mascara: you can make your eyelashes look longer by the way you apply your mascara. First, apply it to the top lashes, then the bottom ones. This gives your top lashes time to dry so you can go back and apply more mascara a second time, which will help them look longer and thicker. And don't forget to apply mascara on your inner and outer lashes. You'll be surprised how full it makes your lashes look.

About special problems on your face: as mentioned earlier, when I was younger I was in a car wreck and had over a hundred stitches in my face which, of course, resulted in scars. I have found that vitamin E oil and cocoa butter can help to minimize those scars. The less you touch facial marks, the better off you will be. That is another reason why a sponge is better than your fingertips for applying makeup.

*Being Your Best:*

The final thing I need to say about taking care of your body is that you have got to be the best you can be on the outside. If you're overweight, get those excess pounds off. If you are not going to do that, at least don't talk about how overweight you are.

If you don't like your hair, get somebody to style it for you. If you're not going to have it styled, at least don't fuss with it all the time.

If you don't like the way your makeup looks, get a friend to do it for you. If you're not going to try to change it, at least don't complain about the way it looks.

I don't mean to sound harsh, but what I'm trying to get you to see is that these things are simple to correct. We all center in on some of the easiest things in the world to be changed. We need to focus on the things that are truly important in life. Get the simpler things, the outside things, corrected; then start your "inner man" growing and let Jesus shine out through you. If you will focus your attention on the important things, all those little things that bother you so much about yourself will be taken care of.

Don't worry about the things that are a problem to you. When you focus on the negatives, you accent them. You need to focus on all your positive features and stop calling attention to your negatives. If you will take the spotlight off the bad and turn it on the good, then the good is what most people will see in you. Try it, it works!

If there are things about yourself that you don't like, and you have the ability to change them, get with it today. Change them. You really need to like yourself. And today is a good day to start doing that. Make a choice to do it. You have it within yourself to make that choice.

But you must *realize* your potential from within. No one is going to do it for you, not anyone! It's up to you! So I want you to go for it. I want you to make the best of everything that God has given you.

*I believe in you, God believes in you, and now you can start believing in yourself.* That's what having a good self-image is all about — delighting *yourself* — in God!

# 8
# Delighting Yourself

My sixth-grade year was a difficult one for me. This was the year that followed the summer of the car wreck. At the first of the year, I hobbled about on crutches. Classmates were attentive and ready to help. But as time wore on, I became more of a burden — it was too much trouble for someone to always have to hang back and help carry my books.

Toward the end of that school year we were learning square dance steps in gym class. More than once during the lessons, I took a fall. But other kids fell too, so it wasn't so bad. However, when the teacher announced there was to be a square dance contest, it put a different light on the matter.

Because of my awkward way of moving, I was late the day the teacher was in the process of dividing the class into teams. As I arrived, I overheard someone whisper, "With Cheryl on our team, we'll never win." Just as any sixth-grade girl would, I felt hurt beyond words.

My mother had sewn new dresses for me, and that evening at home, she announced that we would pin hems after supper. (All my dresses were hemmed to disguise my short leg.)

But I was curt and rude with her. I didn't care about pinning hems. All I wanted was to be like other kids and never have to worry about such things.

To vent my frustrations, I went to the piano to play. But my mind was on the day's events. The situation was impossible. I saw no way I could be anything but a hindrance to the other team members. I wished I never had to go back to school again.

The strains of the happy melody that I was playing were in stark contrast to my depressed mood. I stopped to take a closer look at the music. The words were startling. I stopped playing the piano and began to sing the song *a cappella.*

If you are burdened down with care,
Take it to Jesus Christ in prayer . . .
He can change darkness into light,
When you are lost and cannot see . . .
Jesus will hear your feeble plea . . .
Blessings He will give to one and all,
Who on His precious name will call,
It's really surprising —
Really surprising —
What the Lord can do . . . What the Lord can do.[1]

"He can change darkness into light," I mused to myself. I thought about those words, then I took another look at the mimeographed rules my gym teacher had handed to the teams. The contest was to be judged on originality and skill in two categories: dance and music.

Obviously, I wasn't much good at dancing — but what about music? I'd been playing the piano sinc I was five years old.

---

[1] From *It's Really Surprising (What the Lord Can Do).* Copyright © 1948, 1976 by Albert E. Brumley & Sons.

Quickly I rummaged about our music room and located an old copy of "Turkey in the Straw." Throughout the weekend, with mounting excitement, I formulated an original arrangement of "Turkey in the Straw" along with ideas for the dance steps.

On Monday morning my teammates responded with enthusiasm as I shared my plan. (They were even more pleased when I announced I would remain at the piano while they danced.) Our team practiced hard together and for the first time in ages I felt like my old self — once again a part of what was going on.

On the day of the contest, our team went through our dance without a flaw, demonstrating great teamwork. A shout went up when we were announced the winners. But what followed was the greatest thrill of all. My team gave a rousing three cheers *for me*! It was an unforgettable moment in my young life.

Later as I reflected on the incident, I could clearly see that with God's help, even the most hopeless situation could be transformed into a victory! If I were willing to give my best and turn the situation over to Him, He would honor my efforts. I grasped hold of the fact that I was His child and He wanted only the best for me. And He wants only the best for you. *I had chosen to delight in Him.*

Now am I suggesting that after I learned this lesson as a sixth-grader, from then on delighting myself in the Lord was easy? No, not at all. Just because I chose it once doesn't mean it stuck. The next day was another new day and I had another choice to make, just as you do in your life.

Delighting in the Lord does not come automatically just because as Christians we have Jesus in our hearts. The Lord gives us the right to *choose* the response we will make to obstacles that come our way.

Probably one of the questions I am asked most often by other people is, "How in the world are you happy all the time, Cheryl?" I'm asked that because I truly am happy all the time. Harry says that in my sleep I'm smiling. I used to say, "Lord, I don't understand why I'm happy, but I am." Of course, I've had plenty of good reason to be happy. When you've been healed as I have, you're happy. I've had plenty of good reason to be unhappy too, but I *chose* to be *happy.*

Since so many people were asking me that question, I finally said, "Lord, would You give me a scripture so when people ask me why I am happy I can tell them in Your words why I am?"

He said, "Okay, Psalm 37:4." So I jumped on that and said, "All right, I know that scripture, Lord." (You know how we all love to impress the Lord that we know the scriptures.) So I quoted Psalm 37:4: "Delight yourself in the Lord, and *He will give you the desires of your heart*" — with emphasis on the last part of that quote.

Then the Lord said to me, "Say it just one more time, Cheryl." So again I quoted, "Delight yourself in the Lord, and *He will give you the desires of your heart.*"

Then the Lord said, "One more time." So for the third time I said, "Delight yourself in the Lord, and *He will give you the desires of your heart.*"

Then do you know what the Lord said to me? "Cheryl, you know My part real well!" And I did. Do you know what He said to me then? "My part only works when you do the first part of the verse — your part. *Delight yourself* in the Lord . . . . In fact, the first two words are the ones that make it work: DELIGHT YOURSELF."

Then He began to show me how we, the Body of Christ, have looked everywhere for delight. We have looked to TV; we have looked to our husbands; we have looked to our wives; we have looked to our pastors; we have looked to everybody but ourselves to keep us "up." But God says that that doesn't do us any good if we don't make the *choice* first.

The Lord said, "Delight *yourself.*" He meant, "Do it yourself." After you get a good self-image, then you have to fight for it every day. You may have to make the choice to be happy a hundred times the first day, but the next day it will be easier. Then ten years from now you won't even know why you're happy all the time, because you have chosen it so consistently that it has just become a part of your thinking.

You *choose* to be happy.

My son is just an infant and we call him Happy Harry because he doesn't know that he is not supposed to be happy. He doesn't know that you don't get up smiling, and you don't go to bed smiling, and you don't go around smiling all day long. He thinks that's the way everybody does it, so he does it too.

If you'll look at the first part of Psalm 37, you'll see that things weren't going real good for the Israelites at this moment. They were fretting and worrying, and

David couldn't get them to be committed to the Lord. He talked to them about not fretting and not worrying, but they wouldn't listen. So right in the midst of it all he just threw up his hands and said, "Would you delight yourselves! My goodness gracious!"

That hit me so strongly — that things are not always going to be good. Every possible thing that can happen will happen to try to steal your joy from you. But I have learned over the years that nothing has a right to my delight — nothing.

Now I have been through some hard times and I've been through some good. Early in life when I was told that I would never walk again, I had to make a choice — what was I going to do? I chose to delight myself in the Lord. Then after the Lord performed a miracle and put a bone in my leg where there had been no bone, the leg was still shorter than the other, so I had to make a choice again. What was I going to do? I delighted myself in the Lord, and I called myself a miracle, even though my friends called me a cripple. Then God healed me completely! Oh, I'm so glad I didn't get into self-pity but delighted myself in the Lord instead. If I had not done that, I might still be a cripple to this day.

During those years when I was losing most of the pageants I entered, I learned how to delight myself. You know it can get pretty embarrassing to lose the same pageant time after time. It's not as though I was changing states every year. I was in the same state, entered in the same local pageant, faced the same judges, and competed against the same girls. The judges saw the same dress and heard the same song sung every year. It's hard to keep on smiling and acting as though you're supposed to win when you keep losing over and over. So I learned to delight myself in the *Lord* — not in those pageants or in my winning or losing.

But it didn't stop there. I still have to delight myself *every day*.

Now you may be thinking, "Cheryl, how in the world can I delight myself *every* day?" Well, I asked God the same thing, and here is the answer He gave me.

Read 1 Thessalonians 5:16-18 in *The Amplified Bible:*

> **Be happy [in your faith] and rejoice and be glad-hearted continually — always.**
>
> **Be unceasing in prayer — praying perseveringly;**
>
> **Thank [God] in everything — no matter what the circumstances may be, be thankful and give thanks; for this is the will of God for you [who are] in Christ Jesus [the Revealer and Mediator of that will].**

Well, when God showed me this passage, I saw verse 16: **Be happy . . . .** In other words, "*Choose* to be happy . . ." Now take a look at that. Happiness is an emotion, isn't it? So when you choose to be happy, your *emotions* have to come under subjection.

Then I saw verse 17: **Be unceasing in prayer . . . .** That is, "*Choose* to pray . . . ." Now some people would say that praying is spiritual, but if you are a real prayer warrior you know that many times praying is physical. Your spirit always wants to pray, but your flesh sometimes says: "No, I don't want to pray. I'd rather sleep, I'd rather eat, I'd rather watch TV, I'd rather read." Your flesh will fight against praying. So when you choose to pray, your *body* and *spirit* have to come under subjection.

The next verse says: **Thank God in everything** . . . . In other words, "*Choose* to be thankful . . . ." Where is thankfulness? It's in the mind. So when you choose to be thankful, the *mind* has to come under subjection.

So according to this passage, we are to bring our emotions, our body, our spirit and our mind under subjection by our *choices*.

Now I am a very simple, practical person, and God has to speak to me in simple terms. I have found that 99 percent of the world needs to hear simple things, not profound ideas. Because Monday morning when things aren't going our way, we don't need profound thoughts, we need simple, practical solutions. Personally, I need simple things I can remember, so I know what to do and how to do it. And choosing to be happy is pretty simple.

You and I are the ones who do that. To choose to be happy, you don't have to call anybody on the phone; you don't have to listen to anybody on the radio or a cassette tape; and you don't have to watch anybody on TV. *You* can do it yourself, because God said, "Delight *yourself* . . . ." He wouldn't have told us to do that if we didn't have the power within us to do it.

Again, I'm on a subject nobody likes — personal responsibility for our own actions and decisions. We are called to be responsible for our walk with the Lord — every day and every night, day in and day out. The Lord showed me that when I stand before the Father on Judgment Day and He examines the record books, He isn't going to pull up anybody's record but mine.

I'm not responsible for anyone but Cheryl — *my* emotions, *my* body, *my* spirit, *my* mind.

Now after the Lord showed me that I must choose to be happy, I got to thinking, "Lord, that sounds real good, but it's hard to do. There are many days when I can do this, but there are also days when I can't do it. Lord, what can I do when I just 'flat out' cannot choose to be happy, or I can't choose to pray, or I can't choose to be thankful? What do I do then?"

Then God showed me verse 19 of that passage from 1 Thessalonians 5: **Do not quench (suppress or subdue) the (Holy) Spirit.** That verse just jumped off the page at me, because then I saw that we can choose to allow the Holy Spirit free rein in our lives. So when our emotions, our body, our spirit and our mind can't choose any longer, we can say: "All right, Holy Spirit, I need You right now to choose for me." Then He'll begin to rise up out of us, and (if we will let Him) come out of our spirit and out of our mouth. The Holy Spirit within us will choose to be happy, choose to pray, choose to be thankful — and He will keep our emotions, our body, our spirit, and our mind under subjection. Isn't that great?

Let me ask you a personal question: Do you have trouble controlling your temper? Be honest with yourself. Think back over the events of the past few days. If you know that you have a hard time controlling your temper, look at 1 Thessalonians 5:14 in *The Amplified Bible:* **. . . be patient with everybody** — *always keeping your temper.*

In my Bible I've written out to the side of that verse, "Choose to keep your temper."

You're probably thinking to yourself: "That's easy for you to say, Cheryl. You probably don't have a bad temper."

You don't know how many times as a child I fought with my little brothers because I was angry — and I was bigger than they were! Finally one day I looked at myself and said: "You know what, God? I'm not the least bit like You. I don't even like what I see about myself." Then the Lord let me know that if I would choose not to have that temper, if I would stand on the Word of God and resist it, then I wouldn't have it any more. From that moment forth, every time anger would start to rise up in me, I would say, "I'm not going to get angry." And my choice made the difference.

Some people just don't realize that they *do* have choices to make, and that they *can* make their own choices.

Not long ago I received an invitation to speak to a group of women at Morningside Country Club in Palm Springs, California. When I arrived I knew that this place was different from any I had ever visited in my life. The women there possessed great wealth. I thought, "Lord, what do I tell these ladies?" I was a little bit nervous.

Then I thought, "These people need Jesus just like everybody else does." So I shared with them the same message I've shared with you in this book. God honored it, and those ladies were saved right there in the middle of the day in that rich country club. They were hungry for God.

I remember one little old lady in particular. After the meeting she came up to me and said, "My husband is the president of one of the top twelve corporations in America. In my whole life I have never liked myself; I have not liked my husband; I have not liked my life; in fact, I've never liked one thing about any day that I've lived in seventy years. In all that time nobody ever told me that I had a *choice*."

So I quickly said to her, "Well, I'm offering you a choice right now."

Then with joy in her heart, she said, "I know it, and I'm accepting it. And even though the rest of my life may be short, from this moment forth I realize I have a choice."

I share that story with you so you can understand that God has called us to be obedient, and He has called us to be willing. Granted, there are days when we don't feel like being willing, and we don't feel like smiling, and we don't feel like making the right choices or sharing Jesus with somebody else. But we must realize that may be the one day the other person needs to hear about the Lord. We may be the only person who ever shares Jesus with him. So we cannot afford to let down our guard.

When I sing, "Devil, pick on somebody your own size," I mean it. I have set my heart to declare war against the devil — not every so often, but daily. We must keep the battle going. We must fight as though we were engaged in a life or death battle, because we are. Don't fear the devil! He has nothing on you, if you are walking in the name of Jesus. If you will put on the armor of God and stand firm against the enemy, you don't have a thing to fear.

I have discovered that *praise* is the key to victory. Praise is a choice I make. I have to choose to praise the Lord. I have to choose to lift Him up. I have a saying: "Nothing improves my day like praising the Lord."

A lot of things have happened in my life — some have been wonderful and some have been horrible. But all of them were affected by the choices that I made in my life. I would never have walked again if I had not chosen properly. I would never have won the Miss America Pageant if I had not chosen properly. And I truly believe that the choices that I make today will affect my life when I'm seventy, eighty, ninety or a hundred years old.

The world needs us as Christians to choose to be happy because they're searching for happiness, and only through us can they find the lasting source of all true happiness — Jesus Christ. In school when my friends had trouble, they always came to me. They didn't go to anybody else, even though many of them considered me a little "weird."

I had one pair of blue jeans when I started to college. Obviously my family didn't have much money. On the seat of that one pair of jeans was a big old orange patch which declared, "Jesus Is Lord."

I was reminded of those jeans a few months ago when I went to speak at a great, dynamic church in another city. The girl who picked me up at the airport turned out to be an acquaintance from college who had been totally against God when I knew her. I thought, "Why is she picking me up at the airport, representing this great church?"

I didn't know what to say so I just kind of felt out the ground a little bit. Finally she said, "Cheryl, you probably don't even remember me."

I said, "Oh, yes I do."

"Well," she said, "I remember you too. I thought you were the weirdest girl I had ever met in my whole life. You wore patches on your blue jeans, and you carried notebooks with stickers on them that said 'One Way,' and you were always carrying that Bible around. We got so tired of seeing you coming, so we would talk about you — how weird you were and how you were always smiling."

See, all that time I didn't even know it but I was planting seeds in that girl's life. Every time I walked into the room, she came under conviction.

When I left the church after the meeting, on the way back to the airport, she told me, "Years later I discovered that all you had was what Jesus was trying to get into me. All of a sudden I became weird too!"

I told her she was wrong. "We are normal people," I said, "because we are living the way God created us to live. The other people are the abnormal ones, because they're living in sin."

It just goes to show you that God has a wonderful plan for you. The only way you'll miss it is by failing to discipline yourself and failing to take charge of your life. Put God in the driver's seat of your life and delight yourself in Him.

Isaiah 60:1 in *The Amplified Bible* says: **Arise [from the depression and prostration in which circumstances have kept you; rise to a new life]! . . . .** Have you been kept down by your circumstances? Have your circumstances been so bad that you've fallen flat on your face? Well, that verse tells you what to do: **. . . rise to a new life!** . . . .

The understood subject here is *you*. You arise. God didn't say, "I'm going to come down there and just scoop you up above your circumstances and give you My love, joy, peace, and happiness." He said, "*You* do it. You arise. You delight." And we can do that because He has put His Holy Spirit within us.

Perhaps you do not have God's Holy Spirit within you. If you have a desire to receive Him and the outward evidence, which is speaking in tongues, pray this prayer with me:

"Father, be merciful to me. I believe that Jesus is Your Son, and that He died for my sins, and that You raised Him from the dead. Thank You, Father, for sending Jesus and for forgiving me of my sins. Now I ask You to give me the gift of the Holy Spirit which You promised to all believers. I ask You to fill me with Your Spirit. I pray this in the name of Your Son, Jesus. Amen."

Now you must make a quality decision to control your thoughts. Second Corinthians 10:3-5 tells us to bring into captivity every thought to the obedience of Christ.

Choose to be happy!

Choose to speak positive words about yourself!

Confess good, not bad!

In the Bible there are scriptures after scriptures on being joyful and being happy and delighting in the

Lord. But the one scripture that is the key to happiness, the one that can make your life great through the power of the Holy Ghost is Nehemiah 8:10: **. . . the joy of the Lord is your strength.**

You see, the devil wants to steal your joy, because when he gets that, he has got your strength. You lose all of your power. Then you walk around in a state of depression, or at least without joy in your heart. At that point, you can say good-bye to your strength, because it goes out the door with your joy. So grab hold of your joy. Take control of your own life and decide that choosing to be happy is *your choice*, not someone else's.

One thing I have discovered in life is that most people would much rather have somebody else be responsible for them than to do it themselves. But God has put the *responsibility* for you into *your* hands. You are responsible for yourself. Just because you don't feel like you're in control doesn't mean that you're not going to be held accountable. You will be held accountable even if you're out of control, because God has given you the responsibility for your own attitudes and actions.

What God has called me to do, absolutely no one else can fulfill. What God has called you to do, absolutely no one else can fulfill. And if you are not fulfilling what God has called you to do, it is your fault — no one else's. You must choose to be happy. You must choose to pray. You must choose to give thanks.

I believe that God is saying to us today, *"Do it yourself.* I have done My part. I have made a way for you. I have provided a plan. I have shown you the way. NOW, DO IT!"

God is a good God. He has great things in store for you. But He can't do it *for* you. If He could, He would get saved for you, He would get healed for you, He would get filled with the Holy Ghost for you. But He can't do that because these are *our* choices. God has already made His choice!

He has put within every one of us the ability to have a good self-image, to be a winner, an overcomer, a *be-comer*! You have all His power offered to you through the blood and power of Jesus Christ. Take your rightful authority. Get out there and smack the devil right in the face and take back what he has stolen from you. God has made a way for you. Don't walk — *run* to the light, and as you do, He will make your path straight: **. . . so shall your plans be established and succeed** (Prov. 16:3 AMP).

## My Final Word

It was a long journey from the dusty roads of Choctaw County to the ramp in Atlantic City. I pray that in some way the story of my journey will give you hope that you too can overcome the things that try to steal your good self-image.

Many times I still find myself unconsciously drifting back into old negative thought patterns. But when I recognize these thoughts trying to rise up, I stop and remind myself that this is unhealthy, and I begin delighting myself in the Lord so I can then help others.

Our task is to seek to allow the Holy Spirit to reveal as much of Christ in our lives as He possibly can.

I pray that you understand that when you receive Jesus into your heart, you receive the Spirit and nature of Christ. You must then move on to develop your self-image in Him — or rather, His self-image in you.

A good self-image cannot be developed overnight. But as you choose to delight yourself in God, you will begin to look at the Christian walk as a way of life rather than a destination or goal, because you will continually be fighting the enemy who constantly looks for new ways to destroy your self-image.

Just remember that your heavenly Father wants you to think good, positive things about yourself so you can say good, positive things about others.

By choosing to be happy, choosing to pray, and choosing to be thankful, you can set yourself on the path to becoming the person you've always desired to be — and God will be right there to help and to guide you *every step of the way.*

To contact Cheryl, write:

Cheryl Prewitt-Salem
P. O. Box 701287
Tulsa, OK 74170

*Please include your prayer requests
and comments when you write.*

**Cheryl Prewitt-Salem,** a regular on the nationally televised "Richard Roberts Live" show, has authored three books, *A Bright-Shining Place, Choose To Be Happy,* and *You Are Somebody!;* released four albums and two aerobic workout videos, "Take Charge of Your Life with Cheryl and Friends" (high impact) and "Get Ready with Cheryl and Friends" (low impact) positive self-image encouragers. Cheryl ministers in churches, colleges, high schools and wherever else the Lord tells her to go.

After moving to Tulsa in 1985, Cheryl met and married Harry A. Salem II, Executive Vice-President of Oral Roberts Evangelistic Association and head of the television department. On March 21, 1986, Cheryl gave birth to a wonderful son, "Li'l Harry.".